Collins

11+ Maths

Practice Papers
Book 3

Anne Stothers

Introduction

The 11+ tests

In most cases, the 11+ selection tests are set by GL Assessment, CEM or the individual school. You should be able to find out which tests your child will be taking on the website of the school they are applying to or from the local authority.

These single subject practice test papers are designed to reflect the style of GL Assessment tests, but provide useful practice and preparation for all 11+ tests and common entrance exams.

The score achieved on these test papers is no guarantee that your child will achieve a score of the same standard on the formal tests. Other factors, such as the standard of responses from all pupils who took the test, will determine their success in the formal examination.

Collins also publishes practice test papers, in partnership with The 11 Plus Tutoring Academy, to support preparation for the CEM tests.

Contents

This book contains:

- four practice papers – Tests A, B, C and D
- a multiple-choice answer sheet for each test
- a complete set of answers, including explanations.

Further multiple-choice answer sheets can be downloaded from our website so that you can reuse these papers: collins.co.uk/11plus

Maths

Mathematics tests are used by schools to assess the ability of each child and determine whether they have attained the required standard of mathematical skills, reasoning and problem-solving.

It is particularly important to provide maths practice as the 11+ tests may test skills that are slightly more advanced than those on the national curriculum for your child's age.

The importance of practice

Practice will help your child to do his or her best on the day of the tests. Working through a number of practice tests allows your child to practise answering a range of test-style questions. It also provides an opportunity to learn how to manage time effectively, so that time is not wasted during the test and any 'extra' time is used constructively for checking.

Getting ready for the tests

If your child is unfamiliar with mathematics 11+ papers, it may be advisable to attempt a few questions first without time constraints and give your child the opportunity to ask questions and receive some initial feedback.

It is best to do the tests at a time when your child is alert and able to concentrate fully on them. Tiredness and other distractions will have an adverse effect on their performance. Spend some time talking with your child so that they understand the purpose of the practice papers.

It is also good to go through with your child some tactics to adopt when attempting the paper. These might include:

- Work quickly and carefully through the questions.
- All the questions are worth equal marks, so don't spend too long on any one question.
- If you get stuck, leave it and then come back to it if you have time.
- If you have spare time at the end, go back and check your answers. Every mark counts!

Administering the tests

Make sure that the surroundings are appropriate and quiet. Your child will need a pencil and rubber, and some paper for rough working. A calculator must not be used.

Allow your child some time at the start to read the information on the front of the paper.

Each mathematics test consists of 50 questions to be completed in 50 minutes. It is essential that your child is able to work uninterrupted for this time. A clock should be provided so that a check can be kept on the time left.

Multiple-choice tests

For this style of test, the answers are recorded on a separate answer sheet and not in the book. This answer sheet will often be marked by a computer in the actual exam, so it is important that it is used correctly. Answers should be indicated by drawing a clear pencil line through the appropriate box and there should be no other marks. If your child indicates one answer and then wants to change their response, the first mark must be fully rubbed out. Practising with an answer sheet now will reduce the chance of your child getting anxious or confused during the actual test.

Marking

Award one mark for each correct answer. Do not award any marks for correct working with an incorrect answer, or any half-marks.

It is important that you start by providing some positive feedback for questions that have been correctly answered. This will help your child to identify the topics that they are confident with. Next, identify questions where your child has made an easily correctable mistake or misread the question. Ask your child to try these questions again to see if correct answers can be obtained. Finally, identify the questions that your child provided incorrect answers for, or was unable to answer at all. Revise the material covered by these questions and re-attempt them.

And finally...

Let your child know that tests are just one part of school life and that doing their best is what matters. Plan a fun incentive for after the 11+ tests, such as a day out.

Contents

Practice Test A 5

Practice Test B 17

Practice Test C 29

Practice Test D 41

Answers and Explanations 53

Practice Test A Answer Sheet 65

Practice Test B Answer Sheet 67

Practice Test C Answer Sheet 69

Practice Test D Answer Sheet 71

ACKNOWLEDGEMENTS

The author and publisher are grateful to the copyright holders for permission to use quoted materials and images.

Every effort has been made to trace copyright holders and obtain their permission for the use of copyright material. The author and publisher will gladly receive information enabling them to rectify any error or omission in subsequent editions. All facts are correct at time of going to press.

Images are © Shutterstock.com or © HarperCollins*Publishers* Ltd 2026

Published by Collins
An imprint of HarperCollins*Publishers* Limited
1 London Bridge Street
London SE1 9GF

HarperCollins*Publishers*
Macken House
39/40 Mayor Street Upper
Dublin 1
D01 C9W8
Ireland

ISBN 9780008760625

First published 2026

10 9 8 7 6 5 4 3 2 1

© HarperCollins*Publishers* Limited 2026

All rights reserved. No part of this publication may be reproduced, stored in a retrieval system, or transmitted, in any form or by any means, electronic, mechanical, photocopying, recording or otherwise, without the prior permission of Collins.

Without limiting the exclusive rights of any author, contributor or the publisher of this publication, any unauthorised use of this publication to train generative artificial intelligence (AI) technologies is expressly prohibited. HarperCollins also exercise their rights under Article 4(3) of the Digital Single Market Directive 2019/790 and expressly reserve this publication from the text and data mining exception.

British Library Cataloguing in Publication Data.

A CIP record of this book is available from the British Library.

Author: Anne Stothers
Publisher: Clare Souza
Commissioning and Project Management: Richard Toms
Editorial: Marie Taylor
Cover Design: Sarah Duxbury and Kevin Robbins
Typesetting: Remington (India)
Production: Bethany Brohm
Printed in India by Multivista Global Pvt. Ltd.

This book contains FSC™ certified paper and other controlled sources to ensure responsible forest management.

For more information visit:
www.harpercollins.co.uk/green

Mathematics
Multiple-Choice
Practice Test A

Read the following carefully.

1. You must not open or turn over this booklet until you are told to do so.

2. This is a multiple-choice test, which contains a number of different types of questions.

3. You should do any rough working on a separate sheet of paper.

4. Answers should be marked in pencil on the answer sheet provided, not on the test booklet.

5. If you make a mistake, rub it out as completely as you can and put in your new answer.

6. Work as carefully and as quickly as you can. If you cannot do a question, do not waste time on it but go on to the next.

7. If you are not sure of an answer, choose the one you think is best.

8. You will have 50 minutes to complete the test.

1. Multiply 204.01 by 1000

   A 20401   B 204010   C 204100   D 20410   E 240010

2. Work out the sum of 7629, 45 501 and 8623

   A 20753   B 53130   C 61743   D 61753   E 43753

3. A hexagon is formed from six equilateral triangles.

   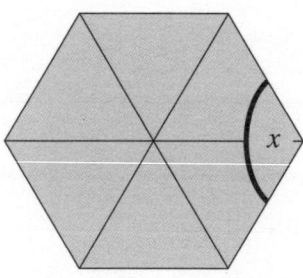

   What is the size of angle *x*?

   A 30°   B 45°   C 120°   D 90°   E 60°

4. Which of these amounts is closest to £20?

   A £17.49   B £23.30   C £22.67   D £17.82   E £17.00

5. Each container below can hold 1 litre of liquid when empty.

   Which diagram best represents a container after 95 ml of water is poured into it?

   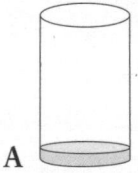 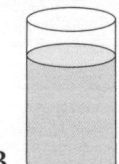 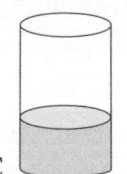 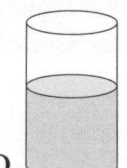

   A   B   C   D   E

6. How many 1 cm cubes will fit into a cube with dimensions 11 cm by 11 cm by 11 cm?

   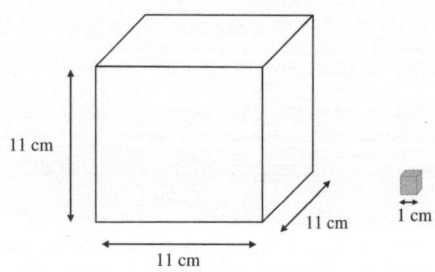

   A 121   B 1331   C 1111   D 11   E 14641

NOW GO ON TO THE NEXT PAGE

7. The diagram shows a grass area with a path around it.

   The length of the grass area is 110 metres, and the width of the grass area is 45 metres.

   The path around the grass area is 1 metre wide.

   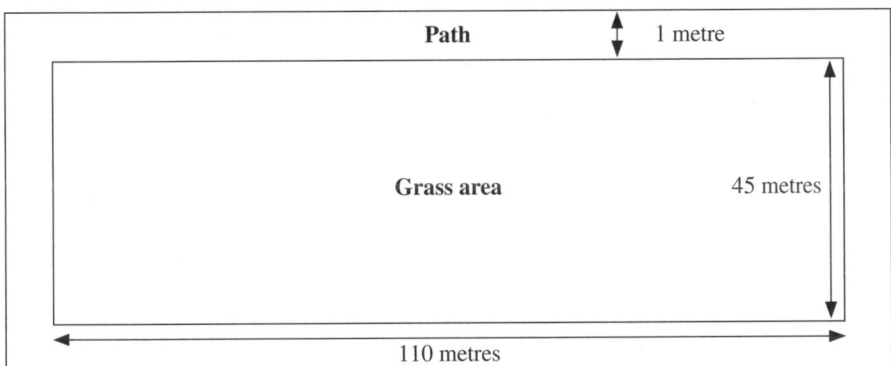

   What is the perimeter of the outside of the path?

   A 318 m   B 310 m   C 155 m   D 159 m   E 314 m

8. Arthur counted the number of people in each car that passed his house one day.

   The bar chart shows his results.

   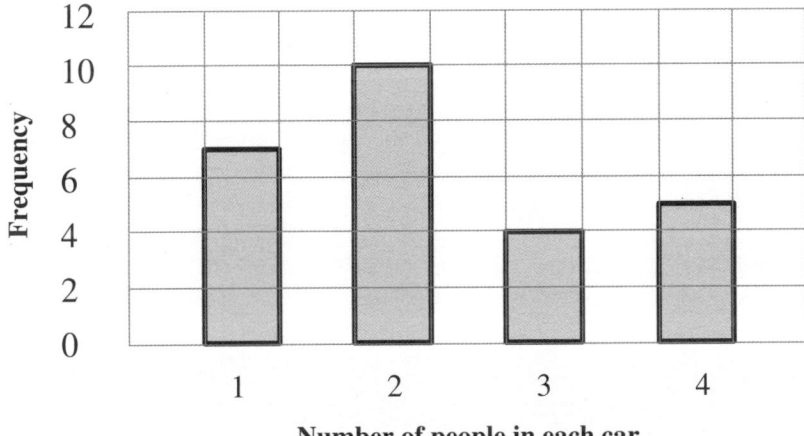

   How many cars did he count with more than 1 person?

   A 9   B 18   C 19   D 20   E 17

9. Molly thinks of a number.

   She multiplies it by 3 and then subtracts 7.

   The answer is 11.

   What is Molly's number?

   A 3   B 4   C 5   D 6   E 7

NOW GO ON TO THE NEXT PAGE

10. This shape is reflected in the dotted mirror line.

    After the reflection, a new shape is made.

    What is the name of this new shape?

    A Trapezium

    B Pentagon

    C Parallelogram

    D Hexagon

    E Octagon

11. What is the next number in this sequence?

    A 4   B 5   C 6   D 7   E 8

12. Eva spends 30% of her pocket money.

    She has £4.48 left.

    How much pocket money did she receive?

    A £13.44   B £14.93   C £5.48   D £8.40   E £6.40

13. Look at the lines shown.

    Which statement below is **not** true?

    A Line A is parallel to line F.

    B Line B is a vertical line.

    C Line A is parallel to line D.

    D Line B is perpendicular to line C.

    E Line C is a horizontal line.

    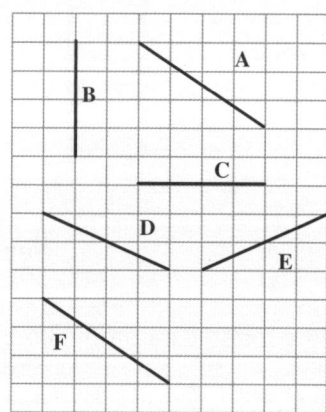

14. Poppy thinks of a number.

    She divides her number by 13, and the answer is a whole number.

    Which of these **cannot** be Poppy's number?

    A 143   B 390   C 1300   D 338   E 1100

15. Calculate the answer to   56.001 − 3.7

    A 55.964   B 52.994   C 19.001   D 52.301   E 52.4

NOW GO ON TO THE NEXT PAGE

16. A piece of ribbon is 3.5 metres long.

    Freya cuts three 40 cm lengths from the ribbon.

    She then cuts what is left into 35 cm lengths.

    How many 35 cm lengths of ribbon will Freya have?

    A 4   B 5   C 6   D 7   E 8

17. Binesh sells cups of squash at a school fair.

    Each cup of squash costs him 15p to make.

    Binesh sells 173 cups of squash for 50p each.

    After paying for the cost of the squash, how much profit does Binesh make?

    A £60.55   B £86.50   C £65.50   D £25.95   E £6.50

18. Work out the difference, in minutes, between 3 hours 40 minutes and $2\frac{3}{4}$ hours.

    A 35   B 40   C 45   D 50   E 55

19. What is the area of the shape below?

    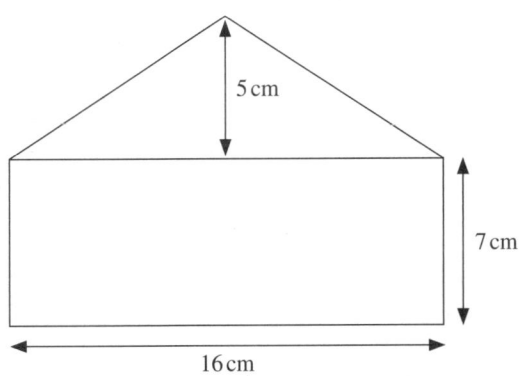

    A 112 cm²   B 224 cm²   C 96 cm²   D 152 cm²   E 560 cm²

20. Work out the size of angle x.

    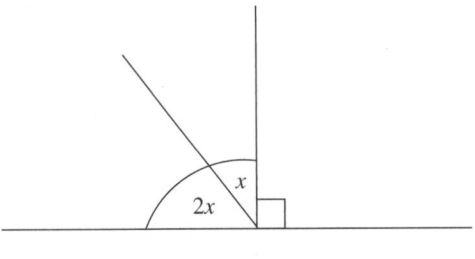

    A 30°   B 45°   C 90°   D 120°   E 60°

21. Here are the ingredients needed to make 16 gingerbread biscuits.

Ingredients to make **16** gingerbread biscuits
30 g sugar
40 g ginger
110 g butter
180 g flour

    How much butter is needed to make 24 gingerbread biscuits?

    A 220 g   B 165 g   C 240 g   D 360 g   E 118 g

22. A group of 35 pensioners were asked if they liked tea, coffee and squash. The Venn diagram shows how many pensioners in total like each drink and how many like more than one of the drinks.

    How many pensioners did not like any of the three drinks?

    A 2

    B 3

    C 4

    D 5

    E 6

    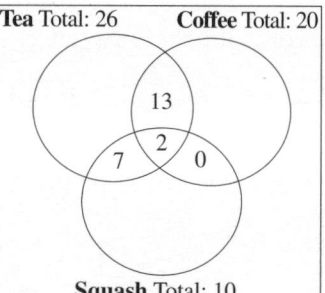

23. In this magic square, each row, column and diagonal adds up to 15.

    Which number should go in the shaded box?

    A 6   B 9   C 4   D 3   E 7

24. Round this number to the nearest tenth.   7.09

    A 8.0   B 7.9   C 7.01   D 8.9   E 7.1

25. 399 people enter a competition.

    $\frac{2}{7}$ of the people win a prize.

    How many people do **not** win a prize?

    A 57   B 114   C 285   D 170   E 297

NOW GO ON TO THE NEXT PAGE

26. The grid below shows four points labelled P, Q, R and S.

    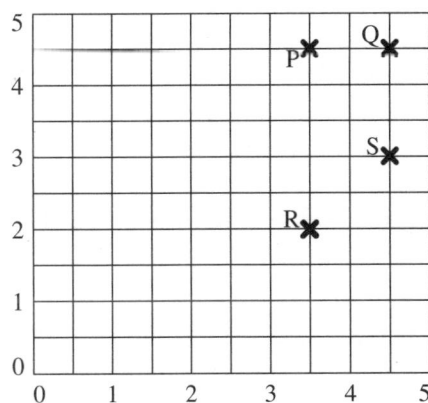

    What are the coordinates of point P?

    A (3.5, 4.5)   B (4.5, 3.5)   C (3.5, 5)   D (4.5, 3)   E (4, 5)

27. The table shows the medals won at an Olympic Games by the top five countries.

Country	Gold	Silver	Bronze
USA	40	44	42
China	40	27	24
Japan	20	12	13
Australia	18	19	16
France	16	26	22

    What is the total number of silver and bronze medals won by these five countries?

    A 128   B 117   C 134   D 245   E 379

28. How many lines of symmetry does a rhombus have?

    A 0   B 1   C 2

    D 3   E 4

    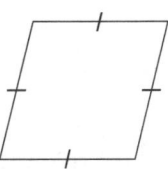

29. What are the names of the three quadrilaterals shown, from left to right?

    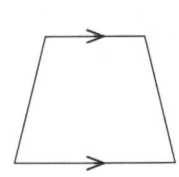 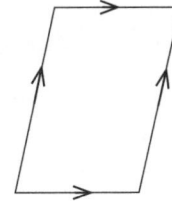 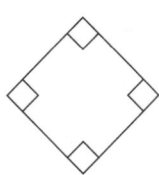

    A Rectangle, parallelogram, rhombus

    B Trapezium, parallelogram, pentagon

    C Trapezium, rectangle, square

    D Square, parallelogram, trapezium

    E Trapezium, parallelogram, square

30. The daytime temperature in Toronto (Canada) on New Year's Day was 1°C.

    By midnight, the temperature had fallen by 7 degrees.

    What was the temperature at midnight?

    A −7°C   B −8°C   C −6°C   D −5°C   E −9°C

31. The pictogram shows the number of people that visited a gallery in the first three months of the year.

    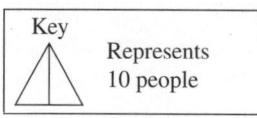

    How many people altogether visited the gallery in these three months?

    A 24   B 110   C 90   D 130   E 120

32. $\frac{5}{6}$ of a number is 8.5

    What is the number?

    A 10.2   B 7.083   C 1.7   D 17   E 9.7

33. A cylinder is filled with oil to a depth of 60 cm.

    The cylinder contains 1800 litres of oil.

    Some oil is taken out of the cylinder and the oil level drops by 20 cm.

    How much oil is left in the cylinder?

    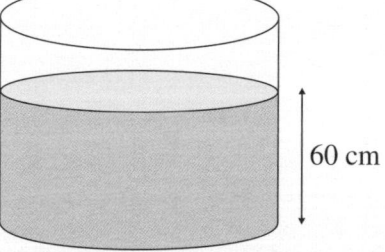

    A 1200 litres   B 1780 litres   C 600 litres   D 1300 litres   E 1250 litres

34. What is the angle between South West and North shown on the compass below?

    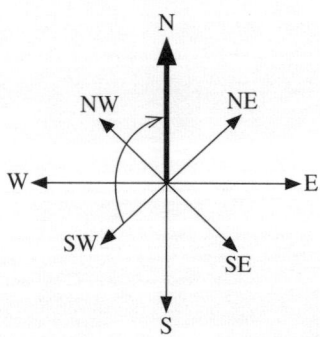

    A 145°   B 120°   C 135°   D 225°   E 95°

35. A coat is reduced from £28 to £21

What is the percentage discount?

A 75%   B 20%   C 80%   D 7%   E 25%

36. Abdi boils a kettle.

The kettle contains 1.9 litres of water.

Abdi wants to make as many cups of tea as possible.

For each cup of tea, he needs 250 ml of water.

How many full cups of tea can Abdi make?

A 8   B 7   C 6   D 5   E 4

37. Mo and Grace saved a total of £378

Mo saved £36 more than Grace.

How much did Grace save?

A £189   B £153   C £207   D £171   E £170

38. A farmer picks oranges and puts them into boxes to sell.

He fits 24 oranges into each box and fills 19 boxes.

How many oranges does he pick in total?

A 456   B 426   C 240   D 114   E 423

39. In 2002, July 23rd was a Tuesday.

On what day of the week was July 23rd in 2003?

A Monday

B Tuesday

C Wednesday

D Thursday

E Friday

40. Two calculators cost £10.40

Three pens cost £3.54

Jo has £200

How much change should Jo get if she buys 30 calculators and 30 pens?

A £6.70   B £7.60   C £8.60   D £6.80   E £8.70

NOW GO ON TO THE NEXT PAGE

41. The arrow on the scale points to the mass of a bag of flour.

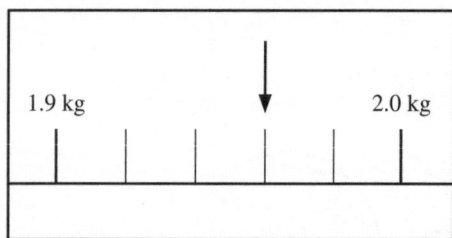

What is the mass of the bag of flour?

A 1.93 kg   B 1.96 kg   C 1.95 kg   D 19.6 kg   E 19.8 kg

42. Multiply 13 by 7.08

A 902.4   B 920.4   C 12.5   D 92.04   E 28.32

43. The graph shows the number of US dollars that could be bought with £1 on five consecutive days.

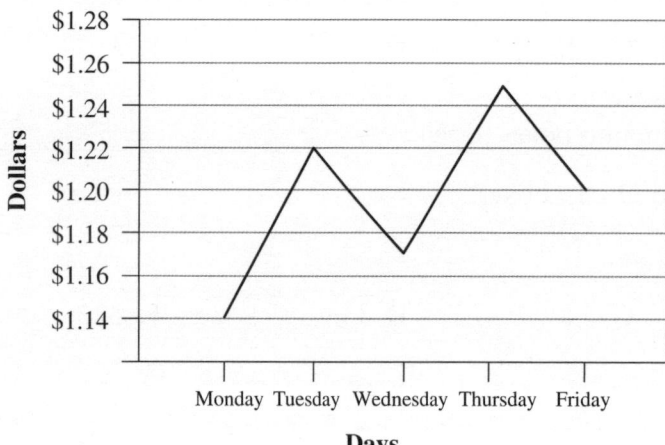

How many US dollars could be bought with £20 on Wednesday?

A $22.80   B $24.40   C $25.00   D $23.40   E $24.00

44. Which of these shapes has eight edges?

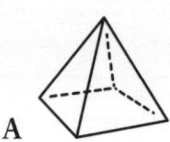 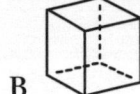 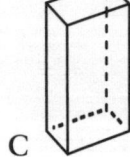  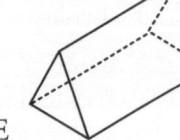

A   B   C   D   E

NOW GO ON TO THE NEXT PAGE

45. This input-output machine divides by 9 and then subtracts 3.

    Input → ÷ 9 → − 3 → Output

    Bella inputs a number and the output is 5.

    Which number did Bella input?

    A 81   B 18   C 36   D 45   E 72

46. Isla has 21 socks in her drawer.

    $\frac{2}{7}$ of the socks are black and $\frac{2}{3}$ of them are white.

    What fraction of Isla's socks are neither black nor white?

    A $\frac{1}{21}$ B $\frac{1}{7}$ C $\frac{7}{21}$ D $\frac{3}{21}$ E $\frac{20}{21}$

47. What is $\frac{3}{8}$ as a decimal?

    A 0.125   B 0.375   C 0.3   D 0.38   E 0.3333

48. Which three prime numbers make 182 when multiplied together?

    A 2, 11, 13   B 3, 5, 11   C 13, 14   D 3, 7, 13   E 2, 7, 13

49. Maths books cost £4.99 each.

    A teacher buys 125 books for the Year 7 students in his school.

    What is the total cost of the books?

    A £632.75   B £625   C £623.75   D £620   E £523.95

50. What is the next number in this sequence?

    4, 6, 9, 13.5, ▢

    A 19.5   B 20.25   C 20.5   D 21   E 18

END OF TEST

TEST ADVICE

This information will not appear in the actual test.
It is included here to remind you not to stop working
until you are told the test is over.

CHECK YOUR ANSWERS AGAIN IF THERE IS TIME

CORRECTING EVEN ONE MISTAKE CAN MEAN AN EXTRA MARK

Mathematics
Multiple-Choice
Practice Test B

Read the following carefully.

1. You must not open or turn over this booklet until you are told to do so.

2. This is a multiple-choice test, which contains a number of different types of questions.

3. You should do any rough working on a separate sheet of paper.

4. Answers should be marked in pencil on the answer sheet provided, not on the test booklet.

5. If you make a mistake, rub it out as completely as you can and put in your new answer.

6. Work as carefully and as quickly as you can. If you cannot do a question, do not waste time on it but go on to the next.

7. If you are not sure of an answer, choose the one you think is best.

8. You will have 50 minutes to complete the test.

1. A transport company is taking some children and teachers on a trip.

   The company has coaches and minibuses.

   Each coach can carry 51 passengers and each minibus can carry 13 passengers.

   The children and teachers going on the trip would fill exactly 3 coaches.

   If only minibuses are used for the trip, how many will be needed?

   A 9   B 10   C 11   D 12   E 13

2. The diagram shows a rhombus.

   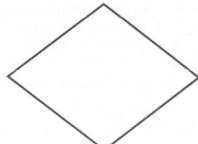

   Which of the following statements is **false**?

   A All angles in a rhombus are always equal.

   B All sides of a rhombus are of equal length.

   C The interior angles in a rhombus sum to 360°.

   D A rhombus has two lines of symmetry.

   E The diagonals of a rhombus cross at 90°.

3. Marni has £10

   She buys a drink for £2.75 and three apples costing 62p each.

   How much money does Marni have left?

   A £6.63   B £6.01   C £2.64   D £5.39   E £4.39

4. What is the seventh term in this sequence?   5, 9.5, 14, …

   A 27.5   B 18.5   C 32   D 23   E 32.5

5. Dawn is currently half as old as her brother.

   In six years' time, Dawn's brother will be 22.

   What is Dawn's current age?

   A 16   B 8   C 11   D 19   E 12

6. By how much is five and one-third greater than three and seven-eighths?

   A $2\frac{11}{24}$ B $1\frac{11}{24}$ C $2\frac{13}{24}$ D $1\frac{13}{24}$ E $\frac{11}{24}$

NOW GO ON TO THE NEXT PAGE

7. A triangle has an angle of 58° and an angle of 56°.

   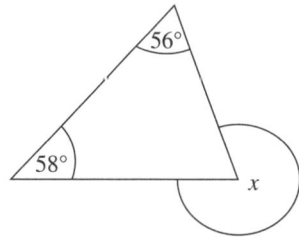

   What is the size of angle *x*?

   A 66°   B 302°   C 294°   D 114°   E 304°

8. A train leaves London at 05:48 and arrives in Inverness at 14:15

   How long does the journey take?

   A 8 hours 27 minutes

   B 7 hours 47 minutes

   C 7 hours 27 minutes

   D 9 hours 27 minutes

   E 8 hours 18 minutes

9. The bar chart shows the temperatures in London and Belfast over five days.

   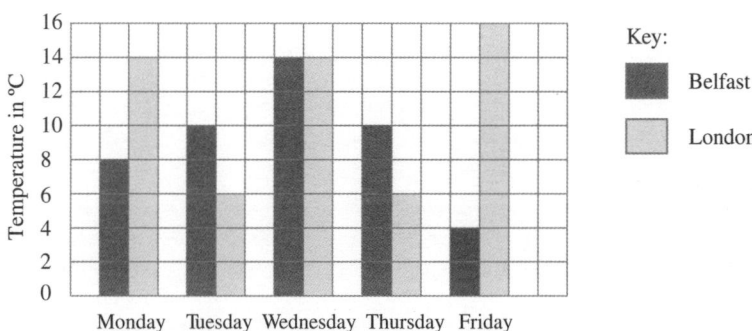

   On which day was the difference between the temperatures in London and Belfast greatest, and by how many degrees?

   A Friday, 6°C

   B Monday, 6°C

   C Monday, 14°C

   D Friday, 16°C

   E Friday, 12°C

10. Alex thinks of a number.

    20% of his number is 64.

    What is 75% of his number?

    A 640   B 256   C 320   D 204   E 240

NOW GO ON TO THE NEXT PAGE

11. Paul has four cards showing the numbers 5, 4, 9 and 2.

    He also has one card with a decimal point.

    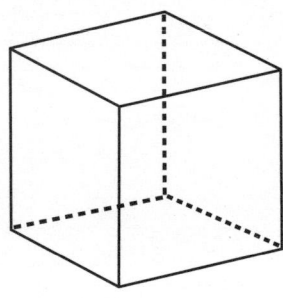

    Using all five cards, what is the nearest number to 50 that Paul can make?

    A 49.52   B 52.49   C 45.29   D 49.25   E 52.94

12. When the lengths of all the edges of this cube are added together, the total is 240 cm.

    What is the length of one edge of the cube?

    A 24 cm   B 12 cm   C 48 cm   D 20 cm   E 40 cm

13. Luca plots the four points given below onto a coordinate grid like the one shown.

    (1, 5) (3, 2) (3, 8) (9, 5)

    He then joins the points to make a shape.

    What shape does Luca make?

    A Parallelogram

    B Rectangle

    C Kite

    D Rhombus

    E Trapezium

    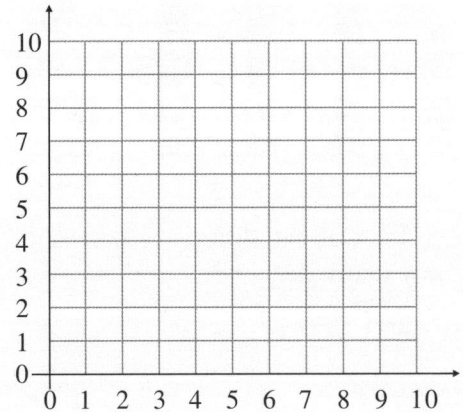

14. What is the difference between the largest and smallest decimal numbers in the box?

    | 0.73 | 0.17 | 0.9 | 0.86 |

    A 0.77   B 0.73   C 0.69   D 0.64   E 0.56

NOW GO ON TO THE NEXT PAGE

15. Work out $0.75 \div \frac{3}{4}$

    A $\frac{3}{4}$ B 1   C $\frac{1}{3}$ D $\frac{1}{4}$ E $\frac{4}{3}$

16. How many grams are in 2.75 kg?

    A 275 g   B 27.5 g   C 27 500 g   D 275 000 g   E 2750 g

17. Mike works from Monday to Friday for 45 weeks each year.

    The total cost of his travel to and from work for one year is £630

    What is his cost of travel for one day?

    A £14   B £2.60   C £1.40   D £2.80   E £3.60

18. Work out the value of ? in the calculation below.

    $\boxed{?} + 7 = -3$

    A 4   B −4   C 10   D 3   E −10

19. The travel graph shows the first 40 minutes of Amy's journey delivering two parcels.

    Amy starts from home and has to stop to deliver each parcel.

    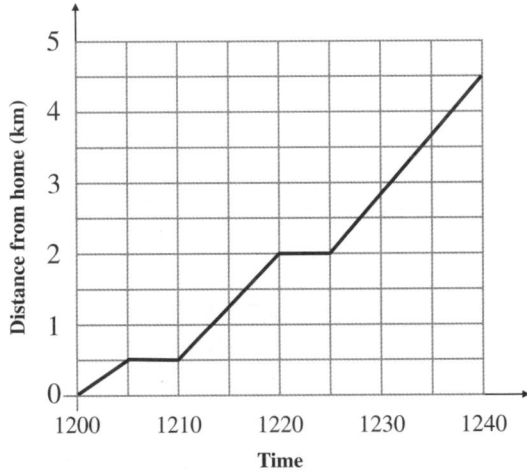

    How many minutes did the two stops take in total?

    A 10   B 5   C 20   D 1   E 2

20. In this magic square, the totals for each row, column and diagonal are the same.

		3
4		8
		7

    Which number should go in the shaded box?

    A 10   B 2   C 5   D 6   E 9

NOW GO ON TO THE NEXT PAGE

21. At a primary school, 16 teachers walk to school, 6 travel by bus and 3 travel by car.

Walk	Bus	Car
16	6	3

    What percentage of teachers walk to school?

    A 16%   B 32%   C 64%   D 60%   E 75%

22. The ages of Grandma, Auntie Flo and Tina add up to 126.

    Grandma is three times as old as Auntie Flo, who is twice as old as Tina.

    How old is Auntie Flo?

    A 84   B 14   C 28   D 18   E 24

23. Harry and George bought identical jumpers from a market stall.

    Harry got a 10% discount.

    George got a 15% discount.

    George paid £1.20 less than Harry.

    What was the full price of the jumper?

    A £24   B £12   C £20   D £15   E £30

24. Which of these calculations gives an answer that is a multiple of 5?

    A $1 \times 2 + 3 + 4$

    B $1 + 2 \times 3 + 4$

    C $1 \times 2 + 3 \times 4$

    D $1 + 2 \times 3 \times 4$

    E $1 \times 2 \times 3 \times 4$

25. Here are five shapes.

    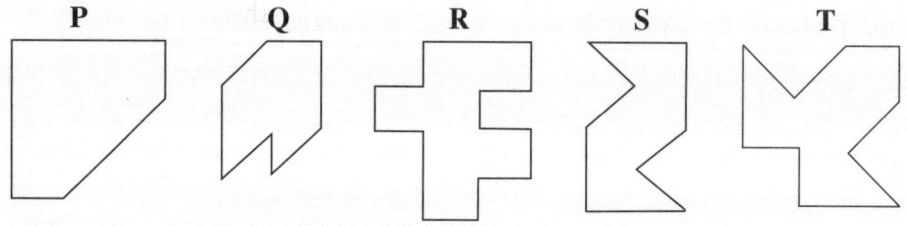

    Which two shapes have line symmetry?

    A P and Q   B P and T   C Q and T   D S and T   E Q and S

26. A group of children were asked which of three flavours of ice cream they liked.

    The results are shown in the diagram below.

    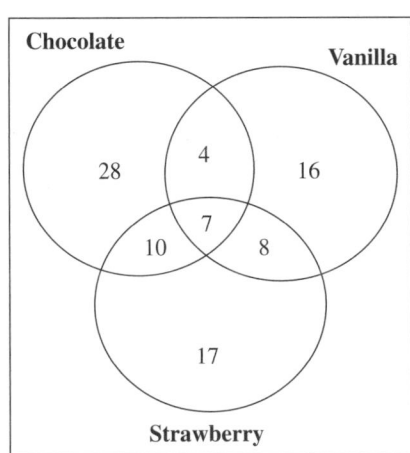

    How many children liked both chocolate and strawberry ice cream?

    A 10   B 21   C 14   D 55   E 17

27. The diagram shows the net of a cube.

    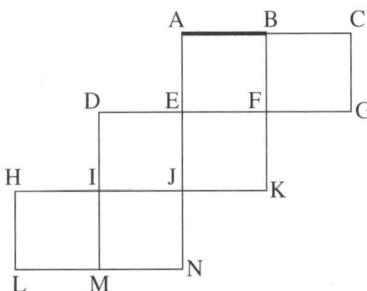

    When the net is folded into a cube, which edge will meet edge AB?

    A LM   B MN   C HL   D JN   E JK

28. The diagram shows a T shape.

    What is the perimeter of the T shape?

    A 31 cm   B 51 cm   C 46 cm

    D 75 cm   E 56 cm

    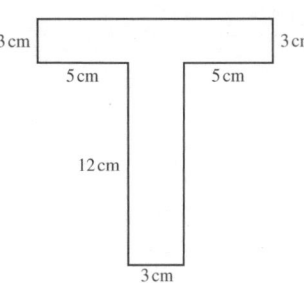

29. The jug contains undiluted orange squash.

    How much water must be added to make 0.5 litres of squash?

    A 450 ml   B 350 ml   C 375 ml

    D 275 ml   E 250 ml

    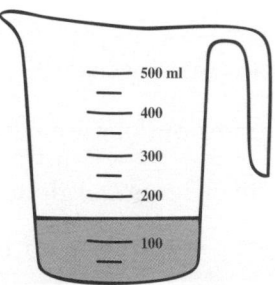

NOW GO ON TO THE NEXT PAGE

30. Sweets cost 12p each or you can buy three for 30p.

Annie has £2

What is the maximum number of sweets Annie can buy with £2?

12p each or 3 for 30p

   A 18   B 21   C 16

   D 20   E 19

31. Work out the volume of the box below.

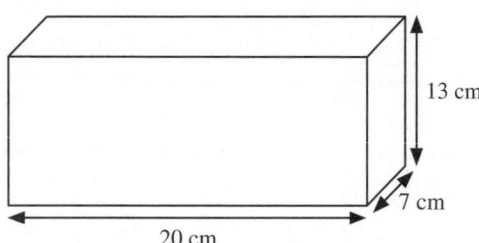

  A 982 cm³   B 40 cm³   C 1820 cm³   D 160 cm³   E 182 cm³

32. How many minutes is the time from 9.23 a.m. until 1.18 p.m.?

  A 231   B 175   C 225   D 236   E 235

33. The diagram shows a regular hexagon.

A regular hexagon is made up of six equilateral triangles.

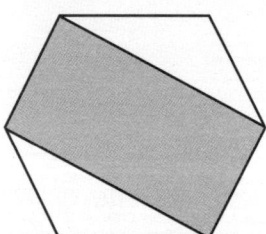

What fraction of the hexagon is shaded?

  A $\frac{2}{3}$ B $\frac{3}{5}$ C $\frac{3}{4}$ D $\frac{5}{6}$ E $\frac{1}{2}$

34. What is the next number in this sequence?

$3\frac{1}{4}, 2\frac{1}{2}, 1\frac{3}{4}, ...$

  A $\frac{3}{4}$ B 1   C $1\frac{1}{4}$ D $1\frac{1}{2}$ E $\frac{1}{4}$

35. Shona is making cakes.

225 grams of flour are needed to make 9 cakes.

How many grams of flour will Shona need to make 20 cakes?

  A 475 g   B 520 g   C 500 g   D 250 g   E 490 g

NOW GO ON TO THE NEXT PAGE

36. 72 children in Year 6 were asked about their favourite fruit.

    The results are displayed on the pie chart.

    Half of the children said 'banana'.

    Estimate the number of children who said 'apple'.

    A 36   B 21   C 15
    D 29   E 32

    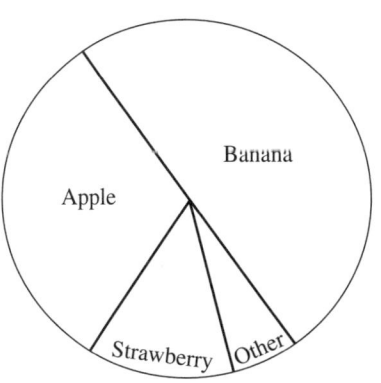

37. Maria buys 7 biscuits at 72p each and 4 sandwiches at £2.23 each.

    How much change should she get from £20?

    A £14.96   B £17.05   C £11.08   D £10.36   E £6.04

38. How much liquid must be added to this container to make 2 litres?

    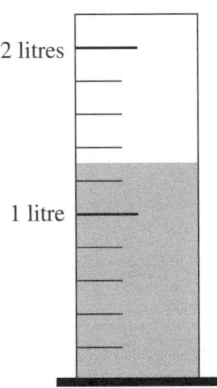

    A 500 ml   B 750 ml   C 0.7 ml   D 700 ml   E 1300 ml

39. Round 36.78 km to the nearest 100 metres.

    A 3680 m   B 3700 m   C 36 780 m   D 36 800 m   E 37 000 m

40. The diagram shows a pyramid. The number in each square not on the bottom row is the sum of the numbers in the two squares it stands on.

    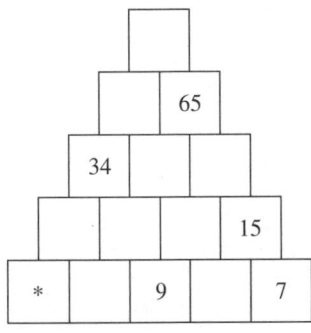

    What number will be in the square marked *?

    A 13   B 10   C 11   D 8   E 7

NOW GO ON TO THE NEXT PAGE

41. Which image shows a reflection of the shape below in the dashed mirror line?

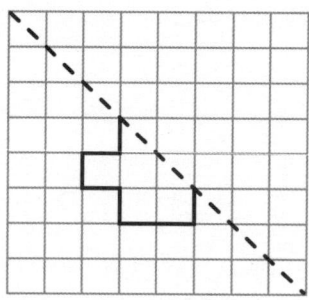

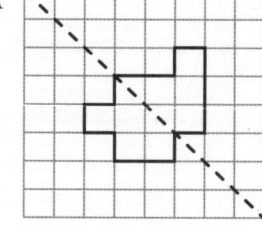   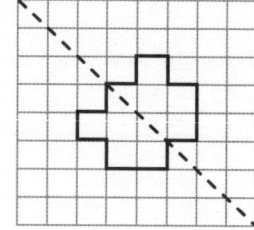   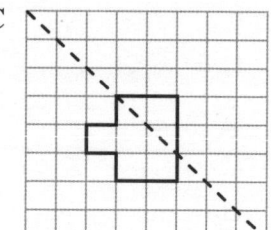

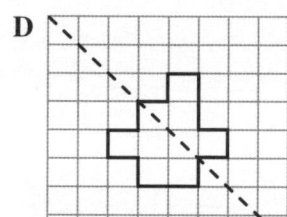   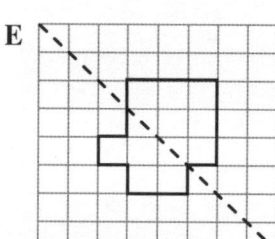

42. Which of these fractions is the smallest?

   A $\frac{1}{2}$ B $\frac{4}{7}$ C $\frac{5}{9}$ D $\frac{3}{5}$ E $\frac{3}{8}$

43. Work out the value of $3 - ((3 + 3) \div 3)$

   A 3   B 1   C $\frac{1}{3}$ D 2   E 0

44. The table shows how many minutes it took four children to get to school one week.

	Isla	Theo	Fatima	Omar
Monday	19	23	13	17
Tuesday	17	26	14	20
Wednesday	21	19	11	16
Thursday	23	22	12	18
Friday	17	24	15	21

On which two days did the four children take the same amount of total time to get to school?

A Monday and Thursday

B Tuesday and Wednesday

C Monday and Friday

D Tuesday and Friday

E Wednesday and Friday

NOW GO ON TO THE NEXT PAGE

45. What is the size of the angle labelled *x* in the diagram below?

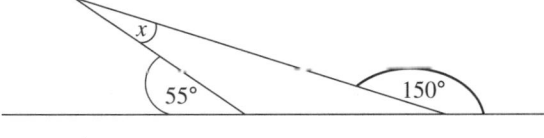

A 35° B 27° C 55° D 30° E 25°

46. What is 30% of 50 squared?

A 750 B 2500 C 250 D 500 E 30

47. The rectangle and the square below have the same perimeter. They are not drawn to scale.

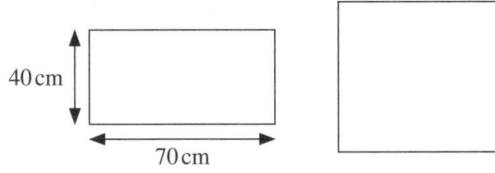

What is the difference between the area of the rectangle and the area of the square?

A 2800 cm² B 3025 cm² C 225 cm² D 756.25 cm² E 775 cm²

48. Which number is seventeen less than two thousand and three?

A 1983 B 2283 C 2013 D 1914 E 1986

49. Which of the following is the best estimate for the length of a bus?

A 0.14 km B 1.4 m C 14 000 mm D 140 cm E 0.0014 km

50. In the word sum below, each letter represents a different digit.

```
  F O U R
  F O U R  +
  F O U R
  -------
T H R E E
```

Which digit does the letter H represent?

A 9 B 0 C 2 D 7 E 3

TEST ADVICE

This information will not appear in the actual test.
It is included here to remind you not to stop working
until you are told the test is over.

CHECK YOUR ANSWERS AGAIN IF THERE IS TIME

CORRECTING EVEN ONE MISTAKE CAN MEAN AN EXTRA MARK

Mathematics
Multiple-Choice Practice Test C

Read the following carefully.

1. You must not open or turn over this booklet until you are told to do so.

2. This is a multiple-choice test, which contains a number of different types of questions.

3. You should do any rough working on a separate sheet of paper.

4. Answers should be marked in pencil on the answer sheet provided, not on the test booklet.

5. If you make a mistake, rub it out as completely as you can and put in your new answer.

6. Work as carefully and as quickly as you can. If you cannot do a question, do not waste time on it but go on to the next.

7. If you are not sure of an answer, choose the one you think is best.

8. You will have 50 minutes to complete the test.

1. The diagram shows a triangle.

   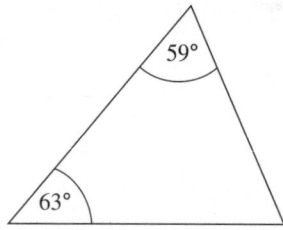

   Work out the size of the third angle in the triangle.

   A 48°   B 63°   C 59°   D 58°   E 238°

2. A bus can seat 53 people.

   5770 people will go by bus to a football match.

   How many buses are needed to take them?

   A 109   B 100   C 110   D 107   E 108

3. A parallelogram has been drawn on the grid.

   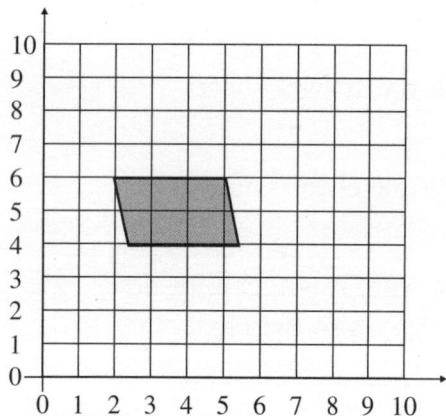

   The coordinates of four points are listed below.

   W (3, 3)   X (4, 5)   Y (3, 5)   Z (5, 3)

   Which coordinates lie inside the parallelogram?

   A X, Y and Z   B X and Z   C Y and Z   D X and Y   E W, X and Y

4. What is 66 ÷ 0.12?

   A 0.55   B 5.5   C 550   D 5500   E 55

5. What is $\frac{1}{3}$ of $\frac{4}{7}$ of 63?

   A 4.5   B 36   C 21   D 3   E 12

NOW GO ON TO THE NEXT PAGE

6. Which of these fractions is closest to $\frac{1}{4}$?

   A $\frac{11}{40}$ B $\frac{16}{60}$ C $\frac{19}{80}$ D $\frac{26}{100}$ E $\frac{29}{120}$

7. Work out the perimeter of the shape below.

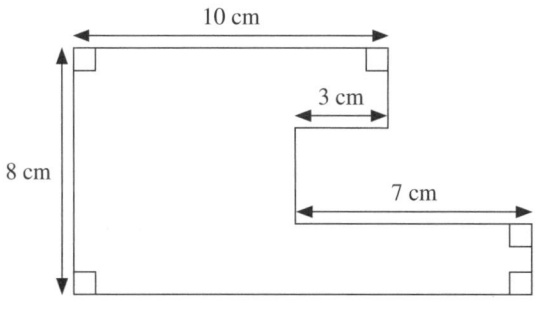

   A 44 cm   B 36 cm   C 28 cm   D 50 cm   E 56 cm

8. Martha has £360

   She gives $\frac{5}{12}$ of the money to her brother and $\frac{1}{3}$ to her sister.

   How much money does Martha have left?

   A £90   B £120   C £150   D £210   E £80

9. Which number between 60 and 80 is a multiple of both 3 and 8?

   A 72   B 63   C 64   D 80   E 78

10. Here is a sequence of negative numbers.

    $$-13, -16, -19, -22, -25, ...$$

    Which of these negative numbers will be in the sequence?

    A −35   B −29   C −41   D −33   E −46

11. Last year, the cost of a bike was £240

    This year, the same bike costs 15% more than last year.

    How much does the bike cost this year?

    A £204   B £276   C £264   D £255   E £286

NOW GO ON TO THE NEXT PAGE

12. Anna asked some people to choose their favourite sport.

    The bar chart shows the results.

    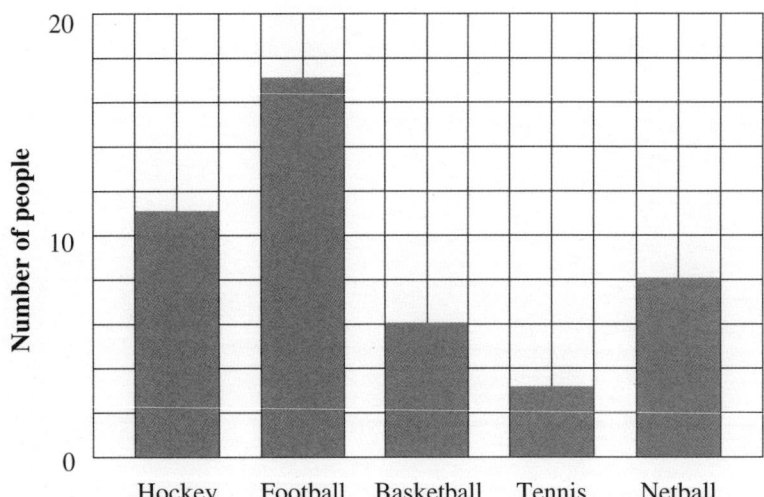

    How many more people chose football than chose tennis as their favourite sport?

    A 13   B 12   C 17   D 14   E 10

13. A bookshelf measures 1.72 metres in length.

    Asha has books that are 5 cm wide.

    How many books can she fit onto the bookshelf?

    A 32   B 33   C 34   D 35   E 36

14. A farmer buys some hens and lambs.

    Two hens and three lambs cost £180

    One hen and four lambs cost £190

    What is the total cost of five hens and seven lambs?

    A £480   B £430   C £360   D £410   E £370

15. The rectangle below has a length 6 cm longer than its width.

    If the perimeter of the rectangle is 40 cm, what is its area?

    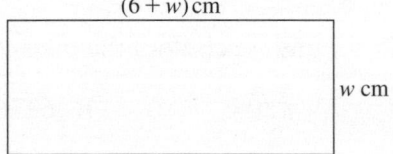

    A 36 cm²   B 72 cm²   C 60 cm²

    D 240 cm²   E 91 cm²

16. Which value is the arrow pointing to on the number line below?

    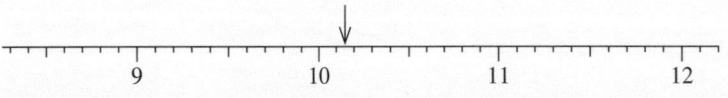

    A 10.1   B 10.2   C 10.15   D 10.05   E 10.5

NOW GO ON TO THE NEXT PAGE

17. The input-output diagram multiplies by 3 and then subtracts 1
    Which number should replace *?

    A 113   B 7   C 9

    D 13   E 23

18. Ravi places 10p coins touching, in a straight line.

    Each 10p coin has a diameter of 25 mm.

    How many 10p coins will Ravi need to make a line measuring 1 metre?

    A 4   B 400   C 50   D 40   E 225

19. Cem has £6 to spend in a shop.

    He buys some items and gets 50p change.

    What fraction of his money did he spend?

    A $\frac{1}{12}$ B $\frac{11}{12}$ C $\frac{50}{600}$ D $\frac{45}{50}$ E $\frac{7}{12}$

20. Add together the following numbers.

    0.507, 65%, $\frac{1}{8}$

    What is the total?

    A 1.282   B 65.632   C 1.407   D 1.957   E 1.237

21. Cakes are being sold at five stalls.

    Stall A is selling one cake for 55p

    Stall B is selling two cakes for £1

    Stall C is selling three cakes for £1.35

    Stall D is selling five cakes for £2.65

    Stall E is selling eight cakes for £4.10

    Which stall gives the best value for money?

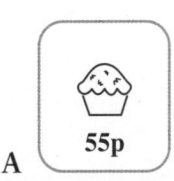 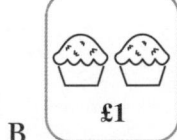   

A   B   C   D   E

22. The rule for generating a sequence is:

    | Double the previous number and add 6 |

    The third term of the sequence is 30

    ___, ___, **30**, ___

    What is the first term of the sequence?

    A 1 B 2 C 3 D 4 E 5

23. A newspaper reports the crowd at a concert to be 17 500 to the nearest 100

    Which number could have been the actual size of the crowd?

    A 17 467 B 17 599 C 17 439 D 18 500 E 17 550

24. A garden centre sells plants at 85p each.

    Molly has £30 to spend.

    How many plants can she buy?

    A 32 B 27 C 33 D 40 E 35

25. Sam is building towers from cubes in a sequence.

    The first three towers are shown below.

    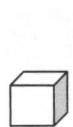 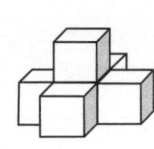 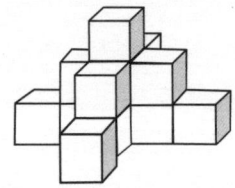

    How many cubes will Sam need to build the fourth tower?

    A 15 B 13 C 22 D 28 E 45

26. The shape below is made up of regular shaded and unshaded hexagons.

    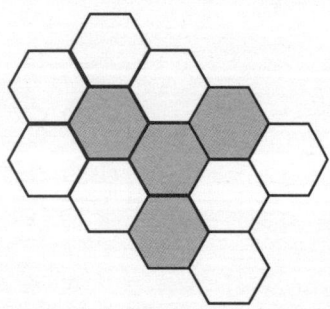

    How many more of the hexagons need to be shaded for $\frac{3}{4}$ of the shape to be shaded?

    A 9 B 4 C 6 D 3 E 5

NOW GO ON TO THE NEXT PAGE

27. A plant was 96 cm tall. It grew by 17 cm.

    How tall was the plant after it grew?

    A 1.13 m   B 1.14 m   C 1.12 m   D 1.16 m   E 1.11 m

28. The table shows the marks scored by five children in Maths, English and Science tests.

	Maths	English	Science
Asif	77	76	80
Billie	67	74	60
Cara	81	84	88
Deepak	60	82	68
Ellie	80	78	64

    Who scored the fewest marks in total in the three tests?

    A Asif   B Billie   C Cara   D Deepak   E Ellie

29. Joe takes his book to a shop to be printed.

    Printing charges

    2.5p per page
    90p for the cover

    Joe pays £6.90 for his book to be printed.

    How many pages are in his book?

    A 276   B 204   C 264   D 190   E 240

30. Amy leaves home to walk to school at 7.37 a.m.

    She walks for 14 minutes to the shop and spends 5 minutes buying a drink.

    She then walks for another 23 minutes to get to school.

    At what time does Amy get to school?

    A 8.16 a.m.   B 8.17 a.m.   C 8.18 a.m.   D 8.19 a.m.   E 8.20 a.m.

NOW GO ON TO THE NEXT PAGE

31. These five numbers will be placed in the Venn diagram below.

    6, 9, 12, 16, 24

    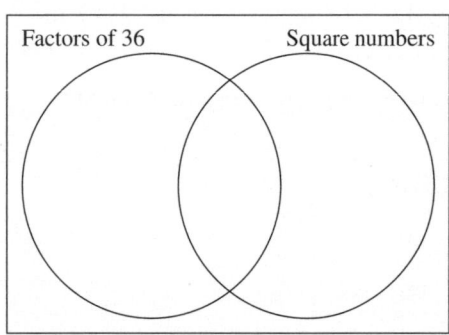

    Which number should be placed in the intersection of the two circles?

    A 6   B 9   C 12   D 16   E 24

32. How many of the triangles can fit into the trapezium?

    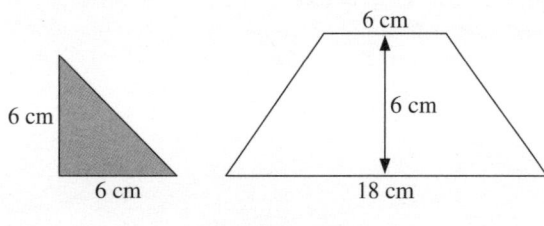

    Not drawn to scale

    A 1   B 2   C 3   D 4   E 5

33. Elliot has 200 sweets to divide equally into 12 party bags.

    If Elliot puts the largest possible number of sweets into each bag, how many sweets will he have left over?

    A 4   B 5   C 6   D 7   E 8

34. Kate is exactly eleven-and-a-quarter years old.

    How many months old is she?

    A 133   B 147   C 132   D 135   E 124

35. A piece of wire 42 cm long is bent into a rectangle.

    The rectangle's length is twice its width.

    What is the area of the rectangle?

    A 42 cm²   B 98 cm²   C 392 cm²   D 72 cm²   E 128 cm²

NOW GO ON TO THE NEXT PAGE

36. The graph below has two points marked on it.

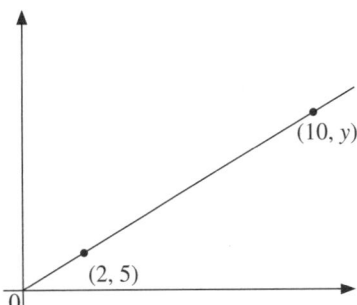

What is the value of *y*?

A 25   B 10   C 12   D 27   E 17

37. Which number is one hundred less than fifty thousand and seventeen?

A 4917   B 50 070   C 51 600   D 49 917   E 41 700

38. 25% of 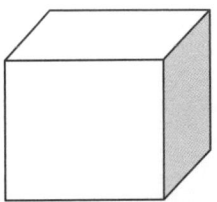 = 16

Work out the value of *.

A 4   B 8   C 32   D 80   E 64

39. The total surface area of this cube is 54 cm².

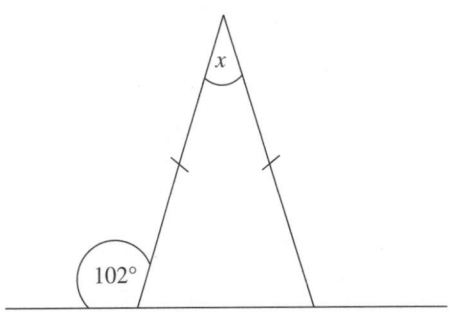

What is the area of one face of the cube?

A 9 cm²   B 8 cm²   C 7 cm²   D 6 cm²   E 4 cm²

40. The diagram below shows an isosceles triangle.

What is the size of angle *x*?

A 48°   B 78°   C 24°   D 4°   E 204°

41. The pie chart shows the results of a football team over one season.

    The team drew 25% of their games. They won and lost an equal number of games.

    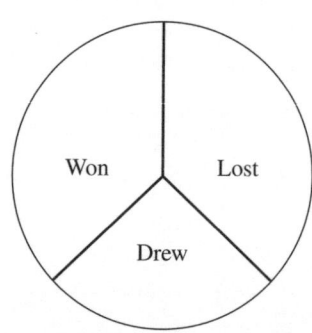

    If the team drew 24 games, how many games did they win?

    A 32   B 24   C 72   D 42   E 36

42. The table shows information about the numbers of squares and circles in a bag of shapes.

    The squares and circles are either red or blue.

    There are no other shapes in the bag.

	Red	Blue	Total
Squares		11	
Circles	8		
Total		16	30

    How many circles are in the bag?

    A 17   B 14   C 13   D 11   E 5

43. Olive's journey to school takes 37 minutes.

    At what time should she leave in order to arrive at school at 8.25 a.m.?

    A 7.58 a.m.   B 7.48 a.m.   C 7.47 a.m.   D 7.12 a.m.   E 7.23 a.m.

44. Rosie has a box of 15 bars of chocolate to sell at a fair.

    She paid £3.90 for the box.

    How much would she need to sell each bar for in order to make a total profit of 50%?

    A 39p   B 26p   C 52p   D £5.85   E 29p

45. Which one of these letters does **not** have line symmetry?

    K   I   L   T   Y

    A Letter K   B Letter I   C Letter L   D Letter T   E Letter Y

46. The diagram below shows two overlapping rectangles.

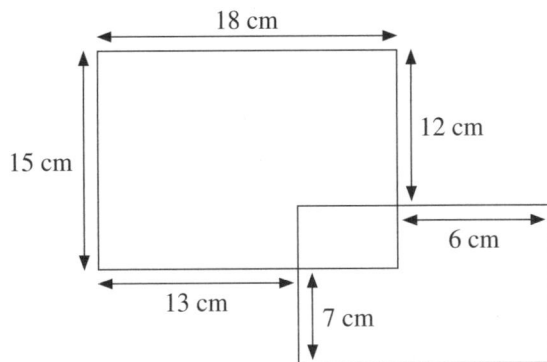

What is the area of the smaller rectangle?

A 42 cm²   B 270 cm²   C 63 cm²   D 110 cm²   E 90 cm²

47. If you are facing East and turn 270° anticlockwise, what direction will you be facing now?

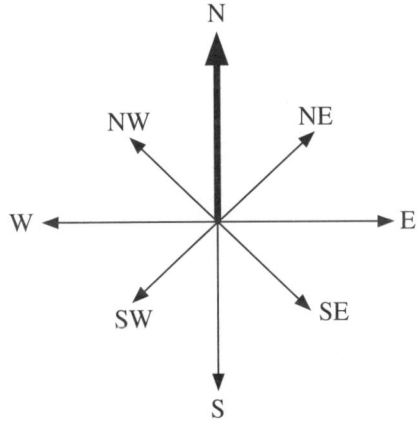

A South   B East   C West   D North   E South East

48. How many right angles are in two complete turns?

A 4   B 16   C 12   D 2   E 8

49. Eva, Mo and Charlie have a bag of sweets.

Eva eats half of the sweets.

Mo eats two-thirds of what is left of the sweets.

Charlie eats the remaining six sweets.

How many sweets were in the bag to start with?

A 12   B 18   C 24   D 16   E 36

NOW GO ON TO THE NEXT PAGE

50. Jack is two years younger than Freddie.

    Feddie is six years older than Orla.

    Jack and Freddie's ages added together are 32.

    How old is Orla?

    A 17　　　　　B 11　　　　　C 15　　　　　D 10　　　　　E 32

END OF TEST

Mathematics
Multiple-Choice Practice Test D

Read the following carefully.

1. You must not open or turn over this booklet until you are told to do so.

2. This is a multiple-choice test, which contains a number of different types of questions.

3. You should do any rough working on a separate sheet of paper.

4. Answers should be marked in pencil on the answer sheet provided, not on the test booklet.

5. If you make a mistake, rub it out as completely as you can and put in your new answer.

6. Work as carefully and as quickly as you can. If you cannot do a question, do not waste time on it but go on to the next.

7. If you are not sure of an answer, choose the one you think is best.

8. You will have 50 minutes to complete the test.

1. What is the number seven million, sixty-five thousand and twenty-eight written in figures?

   A 7 650 028 B 7 065 280 C 7 065 028 D 7 650 280 E 7 006 528

2. What is the smaller angle between the hands of a clock at 12.30?

   A 195° B 25° C 170° D 150° E 165°

3. The distance from Paris to Calais is 320 km.

   5 miles is approximately equal to 8 kilometres.

   Work out the approximate distance in miles from Paris to Calais.

   A 512 miles B 200 miles C 40 miles D 400 miles E 220 miles

4. Dress material costs £10.06 per metre.

   How much will it cost to buy 10 metres?

   A £100.60 B £106.00 C £1006.00 D £10 060 E £160.00

5. Work out $-16 + (-3)^2$

   A −25 B −19 C −13 D −7 E 7

6. Riaz uses this rule to write a sequence:

   | Triple the previous number and then subtract 2 |

   Riaz's sequence begins:

   3, 7, 19, …

   What is the next number in his sequence?

   A 48 B 55 C 36 D 57 E 45

NOW GO ON TO THE NEXT PAGE

7. In 2024, the population of the UK was 69 140 000.

   In 2024, the population of London was 9 650 000.

   Which is closest to the percentage of the UK population in London?

   A 10%   B 20%   C 5%   D 15%   E 7%

8. Minah gave each of her friends one-twelfth of her sweets.

   She had one-third of her sweets left over.

   How many friends did Minah give her sweets to?

   A 8   B 12   C 9   D 6   E 4

9. The diagram shows an octagonal prism.

   The sides are made up of glass rectangles.

   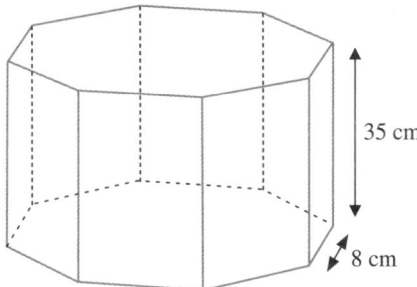

   What area of glass is needed to make all eight of the sides?

   A 2420 cm²   B 280 cm²   C 1680 cm²   D 17 920 cm²   E 2240 cm²

10. A puppy has a mass of 3 kg to the nearest 100 g.

    Which pair of numbers correctly completes this sentence?

    The actual mass of the puppy is between _____ kg and _____ kg.

    A 2.995 and 3.005

    B 2.99 and 3.01

    C 2.95 and 3.05

    D 2.5 and 3.5

    E 2.9 and 3.1

NOW GO ON TO THE NEXT PAGE

11. The sum of three whole numbers is 1500

    One of the numbers is between 775 and 825

    Another of the numbers is between 125 and 175

    Which of these could be the third number?

    A 418   B 683   C 539   D 752   E 338

12. What is $\frac{51}{60}$ written as a decimal?

    A 0.85   B 0.8   C 0.51   D 0.6   E 0.75

13. A map has a scale of 1 cm : 6 km.

    On the map, the distance between two towns is 5.5 cm.

    What is the real-life distance between the two towns?

    A 5.5 km   B 55 km   C 27.5 km   D 33 km   E 30 km

14. There are twice as many girls as boys in a tennis club.

    If there are a total of 96 children in the tennis club, how many of them are girls?

    A 32   B 64   C 48   D 24   E 60

15. The table below gives information about the nutrition in 100 grams of almonds.

100 g contains:	
Protein	21.15 g
Fat	49.93 g
Carbohydrates	21.55 g
Fibre	12.50 g
Sugar	4.35 g

    How many grams of fibre are there in 1 kilogram of almonds?

    A 1250 g   B 1.25 g   C 125 g   D 0.125 g   E 25 g

16. What value is the arrow pointing to on this scale?

    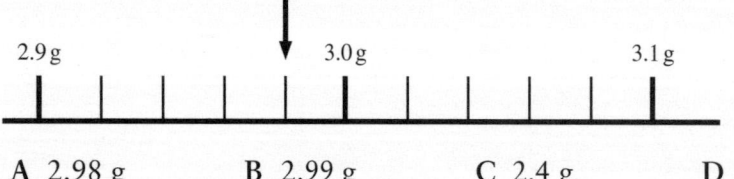

    A 2.98 g   B 2.99 g   C 2.4 g   D 2.13 g   E 2.95 g

17. Which shape contains a reflex angle?

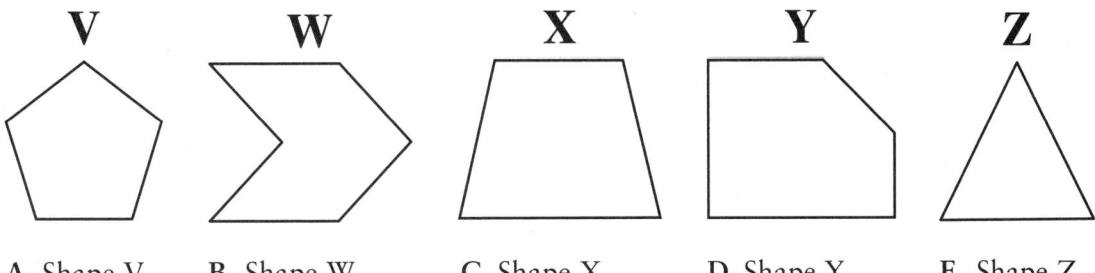

   A Shape V   B Shape W   C Shape X   D Shape Y   E Shape Z

18. Lena is making fruit smoothies.

    The pictogram shows information about the fruit she has.

    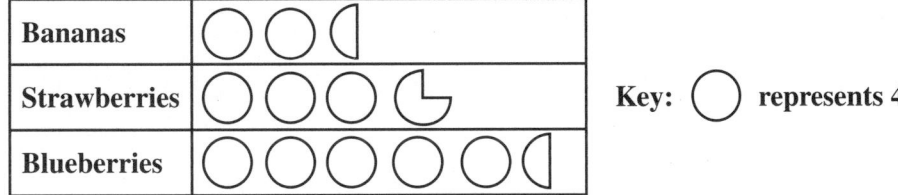

    The ingredients for one fruit smoothie are:

    Fruit smoothie recipe
    $1\frac{1}{2}$ bananas
    4 strawberries
    5 blueberries

    What is the maximum number of fruit smoothies Lena can make?

    A 4   B 3   C 6   D 5   E 7

19. Leon is stacking cans of tomato soup for display in a supermarket.

    He uses 10 cans for the first four rows, as shown in the diagram.

    If his final display has 28 cans, how many rows are needed?

    A 6   B 8   C 5   D 9   E 7

NOW GO ON TO THE NEXT PAGE

20. Some children were asked whether they had visited France, Germany or Spain.

    The information was put into this Venn diagram.

    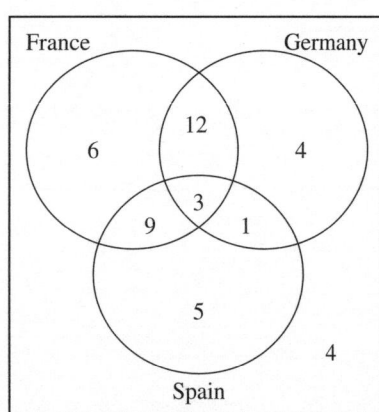

    What fraction of the children had visited France and Spain?

    A $\frac{9}{40}$　　　　B $\frac{9}{44}$　　　　C $\frac{1}{4}$　　　　D $\frac{3}{11}$　　　　E $\frac{1}{3}$

21. Jack uses 1 cm cubes to make a large cube with sides of 3 cm, as shown below.

    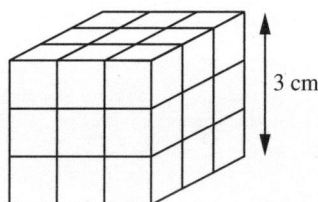

    How many 1 cm cubes does Jack need to make this large cube?

    A 27　　　　B 9　　　　C 81　　　　D 54　　　　E 18

22. Mr Smith buys eight doughnuts.

    Each doughnut costs £1.46

    Mr Smith pays with a £20 note.

    How much change should he get?

    A £11.24　　　　B £11.68　　　　C £8.32　　　　D £9.42　　　　E £8.42

23. Work out the size of angle x in the diagram below.

    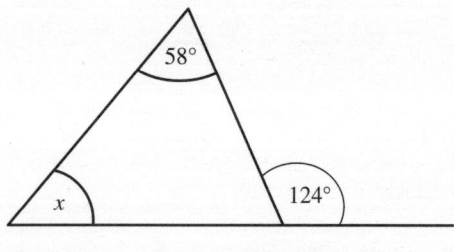

    A 58°　　　　B 56°　　　　C 76°　　　　D 68°　　　　E 66°

NOW GO ON TO THE NEXT PAGE

24. At a summer camp, children can choose two sports each day.

    They can choose from this list of sports:

Sports Choices
1. Football
2. Swimming
3. Hockey
4. Netball
5. Basketball
6. Golf

    The children can choose the same sport or different sports.

    How many different combinations of sports does the summer camp offer each day?

    A 30   B 24   C 15   D 36   E 21

25. The graph shows the science and maths scores of five students.

    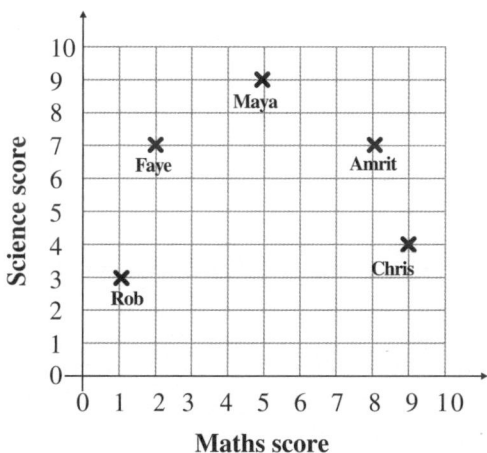

    Who had the highest score in maths?

    A Chris   B Rob   C Faye   D Maya   E Amrit

26. There are a total of 39 dogs and cats in an animal rescue centre.

    Which one of these statements **cannot** be true?

    A There are more dogs than cats in the rescue centre.

    B There are more cats than dogs in the rescue centre.

    C There are five more dogs than cats in the rescue centre.

    D There are three more cats than dogs in the rescue centre.

    E There are two more cats than dogs in the rescue centre.

NOW GO ON TO THE NEXT PAGE

27. Ravi wants to guide a robot along the shaded squares through the maze.

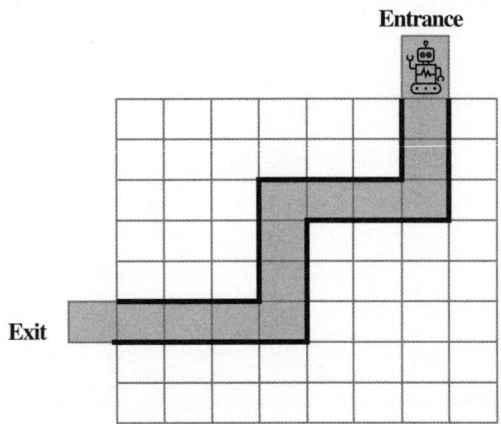

The robot starts on the square marked 'Entrance' and must finish on the square marked 'Exit'.

The robot can only move FORWARD, TURN RIGHT 90° and TURN LEFT 90°.

Which instructions will guide the robot through the maze?

A FORWARD 3, TURN LEFT 90°, FORWARD 3, TURN RIGHT 90°, FORWARD 3, TURN LEFT 90°, FORWARD 4

B FORWARD 2, TURN RIGHT 90°, FORWARD 3, TURN LEFT 90°, FORWARD 3, TURN LEFT 90°, FORWARD 4

C FORWARD 3, TURN RIGHT 90°, FORWARD 3, TURN RIGHT 90°, FORWARD 2, TURN RIGHT 90°, FORWARD 4

D FORWARD 3, TURN RIGHT 90°, FORWARD 3, TURN LEFT 90°, FORWARD 3, TURN RIGHT 90°, FORWARD 4

E FORWARD 2, TURN RIGHT 90°, FORWARD 3, TURN LEFT 90°, FORWARD 3, TURN RIGHT 90°, FORWARD 3

28. If these fractions were ordered from smallest to largest, which fraction would be in the middle position?

$\frac{3}{7}$ $\frac{5}{9}$ $\frac{15}{16}$ $\frac{1}{4}$ $\frac{7}{8}$

A $\frac{3}{7}$ **B** $\frac{5}{9}$ **C** $\frac{15}{16}$ **D** $\frac{1}{4}$ **E** $\frac{7}{8}$

29. Look at this number machine.

Z → ×7 → −7 → ÷4 → ?

If the final number is 7, what is the value of Z?

A 10   **B** 7   **C** 5   **D** 3   **E** 147

30. The diagram shows a regular octagon.

    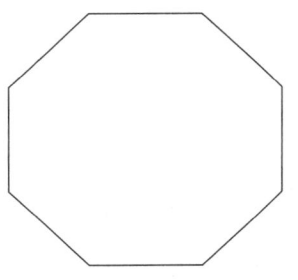

    How many pairs of parallel lines are there altogether in the diagram?

    A 8 　　B 3 　　C 2 　　D 0 　　E 4

31. The arrow is pointing to the speed a car is travelling in km/h.

    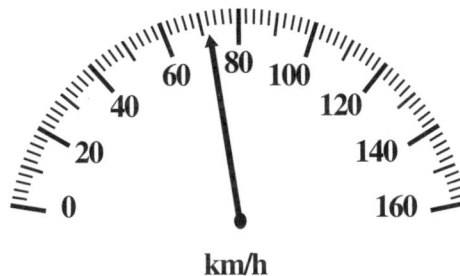

    If the car speeds up by 10 km/h, how fast will it be travelling?

    A 76 km/h 　　B 82 km/h 　　C 86 km/h 　　D 81 km/h 　　E 80 km/h

32. A bag of fertiliser costs £3.50 and it will cover 6 square metres of garden.

    What is the cost of covering a garden measuring 6.5 metres by 4 metres?

    A £14 　　B £15.17 　　C £17.50 　　D £7 　　E £16.50

33. Sarah sells 97 raffle tickets for 25p each.

    How much does she sell the tickets for in total?

    A £24 　　B £24.50 　　C £24.75 　　D £24.25 　　E £23.25

34. Freya starts at 0 and counts up in steps of $2\frac{1}{3}$

    Which of these numbers is in her sequence?

    A 6 　　B 7 　　C 8 　　D 9 　　E 10

35. How many vertices does a cuboid have?

    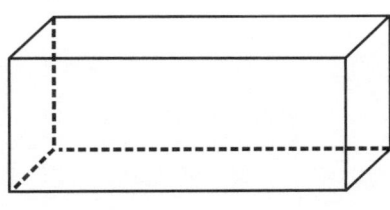

    A 8 　　B 4 　　C 6 　　D 12 　　E 10

NOW GO ON TO THE NEXT PAGE

36. The table below shows information about some children in a class.

		Eye colour		
		Brown	Green	Blue
Wears glasses	Yes	1	3	4
	No	?	6	5

If there are 27 children in the class, which number is missing from the table?

A 4   B 5   C 6   D 7   E 8

37. Kate, Jenny and Alex all started a puzzle at the same time.

Kate completed the puzzle in 6 minutes 23 seconds.

Jenny completed the same puzzle 2 minutes 40 seconds after Kate.

Alex completed the puzzle 3 minutes 16 seconds before Jenny.

How long did Alex take to complete the puzzle?

A 6 minutes and 47 seconds

B 6 minutes and 57 seconds

C 5 minutes and 19 seconds

D 5 minutes and 47 seconds

E 6 minutes and 45 seconds

38. The shoe sizes of some children are recorded and displayed on a bar chart.

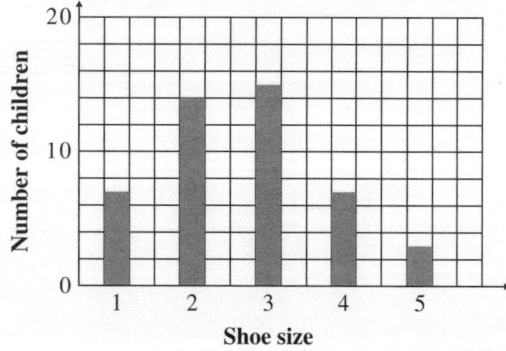

How many children are represented in the bar chart?

A 40   B 23   C 46   D 15   E 39

39. Which of these calculations gives the **smallest** answer?

A 24 × 23 + 27 − 26

B 27 × 26 + 25 − 24

C 23 × 26 + 25 − 27

D 25 × 24 + 23 − 27

E 23 × 24 + 26 − 27

40. Add together $\frac{3}{4} + 0.2 + \frac{39}{50}$

    Which is the correct answer?

    A 1.16   B 1.73   C 1.34   D 1.55   E 1.05

41. The triangle is reflected in the dashed mirror line.

    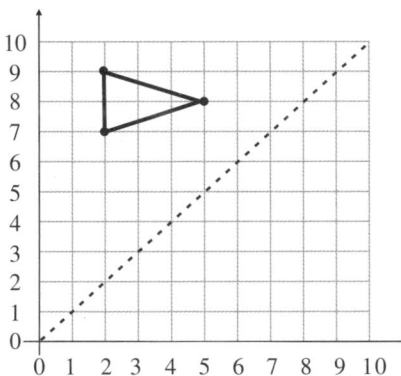

    What are the coordinates of the reflected triangle?

    A (7, 2) (9, 2) (8, 5)

    B (6, 3) (9, 2) (9, 4)

    C (5, 2) (8, 1) (8, 3)

    D (4, 1) (4, 3) (7, 2)

    E (2, 7) (2, 9) (5, 8)

42. A quadrilateral is shown.

    What is the size of angle *x*?

    A 37°   B 143°   C 127°

    D 172°   E 53°

    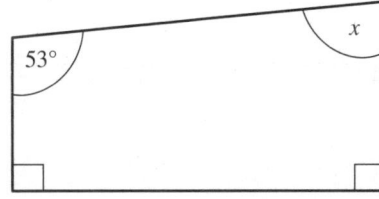

43. The diagram shows four identical rectangles placed around a shaded square.

    Each rectangle is 15 cm long and 5 cm wide.

    What is the area of the shaded square?

    A 100 cm²   B 225 cm²   C 25 cm²

    D 400 cm²   E 40 cm²

    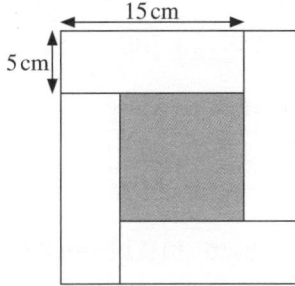

44. One mile is $\frac{8}{5}$ kilometres.

    How many kilometres are equal to 10 miles?

    A 40 km   B 20 km   C 8 km   D 24 km   E 16 km

45. The sum of the first four prime numbers is 17.

    What is the sum of the first five prime numbers?

    A 26   B 30   C 19   D 23   E 28

46. Aygul buys five identical pens.

    She pays with a £20 note and her change is £9.30

    How much will three of the same pens cost?

    A £2.14   B £5.58   C £6.42   D £4.50   E £6.30

47. A rectangle has a perimeter of 32 cm.

    Which of these **cannot** be the area of the rectangle?

    A 60 cm²   B 36 cm²   C 48 cm²   D 39 cm²   E 15 cm²

48. This shape is a square-based pyramid.

    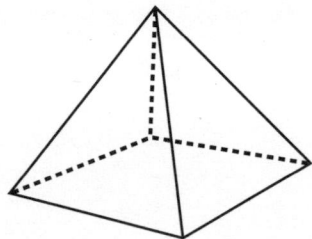

    Which of these is **not** a possible net of the square-based pyramid?

    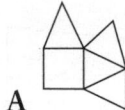 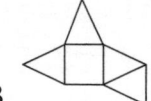 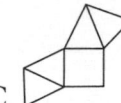 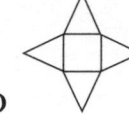

    A   B   C   D   E

49. Which of these is different in value from the others?

    A 50% of 96

    B 75% of 64

    C 15% of 360

    D 25% of 192

    E 60% of 80

50. Jacob ate 110 blueberries in five days.

    Each day he ate 8 more blueberries than the day before.

    How many blueberries did he eat on the last day?

    A 48   B 26   C 42   D 38   E 36

END OF TEST

Collins
PRACTICE PAPERS

Answers and Explanations

Mathematics

Practice Test A Answers and Explanations

1. **B 204 010**
   204.01 × 1000 = 204 010
2. **D 61 753**
   7629 + 45 501 + 8623 = 61 753
3. **C 120°**
   There are 180° in a triangle. Equilateral triangles have equal angles, so each interior angle in an equilateral triangle is 60°.
   2 × 60° = 120°
4. **D £17.82**
   £20 − £17.49 = £2.51
   £23.30 − £20 = £3.30
   £22.67 − £20 = £2.67
   £20 − £17.82 = £2.18
   £20 − £17 = £3
5. **A**
   There are 1000 ml in 1 litre, so 95 ml will fill just under $\frac{1}{10}$ of the container $\left(\frac{100 \text{ ml}}{1000 \text{ ml}} = \frac{1}{10}\right)$. Diagram A shows this best.
6. **B 1331**
   The bottom layer of the cube will fit 11 × 11 = 121 small cubes.
   The large cube is 11 cm high so there will be 11 layers of small cubes.
   121 × 11 = 1331 small cubes in total.
7. **A 318 m**
   The length of the outside of the path will measure 2 metres more than the length of the grass area as the path is 1 metre in width all the way around.
   The width of the outside of the path will also measure 2 metres more than the width of the grass area.
   110 m + 2 m = 112 m
   (length of outside of path)
   45 m + 2 m = 47 m
   (width of outside of path)
   Perimeter of outside of path will be
   112 m + 112 m + 47 m + 47 m = 318 m
8. **C 19**
   10 cars had 2 people, 4 cars had 3 people and 5 cars had 4 people.
   10 + 4 + 5 = 19, so altogether 19 cars had more than 1 person.
9. **D 6**
   Working backwards:
   11 + 7 = 18
   18 ÷ 3 = 6
10. **B Pentagon**

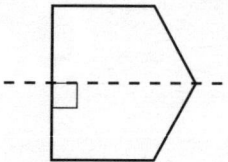

11. **D 7**
    The term-to-term rule of the sequence is add 4.
    3 + 4 = 7
12. **E £6.40**
    £4.48 represents 100 − 30 = 70% of Eva's pocket money.
    If 70% = £4.48,
    then 10% = £4.48 ÷ 7 = £0.64 (64p)
    This means that Eva's pocket money (100%) was £0.64 × 10 = £6.40
13. **C Line A is parallel to line D**
14. **E 1100**
    The only number in the list not divisible by 13 is 1100.
15. **D 52.301**
    Add extra zeros to help with place value.
    56.001 − 3.700 = 52.301
16. **C 6**
    3.5 metres = 350 cm
    350 cm − (3 × 40 cm) =
    350 cm − 120 cm = 230 cm
    left after the 40 cm lengths are cut.
    230 ÷ 35 = 6 remainder 20 cm
17. **A £60.55**
    Binesh makes 50p − 15p = 35p profit on each cup of squash.
    173 × 35 = 6055p = £60.55
18. **E 55**
    3 hours 40 minutes
    = 3 × 60 + 40 = 220 minutes
    $2\frac{3}{4}$ hours = 2 × 60 + 45 = 120 + 45 = 165 minutes
    220 − 165 = 55 minutes difference
19. **D 152 cm²**
    The area of the rectangle is
    16 cm × 7 cm = 112 cm²
    The area of the triangle is
    16 cm × 5 cm ÷ 2 = 40 cm²
    Total area is 112 cm² + 40 cm² = 152 cm²
20. **A 30°**
    Angles on a straight line equal 180°.
    The right-angle equals 90°,
    leaving $x + 2x = 90°$.
    $3x = 90°$.
    Therefore $x = 90° ÷ 3 = 30°$

21. **B 165 g**
    110 g butter makes 16 biscuits so 55 g would make 8 biscuits.
    16 + 8 = 24 so the amount of butter required is 110 g + 55 g = 165 g
22. **B 3**
    26 − 13 − 7 − 2 = 4 like tea only
    20 − 13 − 2 − 0 = 5 like coffee only
    10 − 7 − 2 − 0 = 1 likes squash only
    4 + 5 + 1 + 13 + 7 + 2 + 0 = 32
    35 − 32 = 3
23. **D 3**

    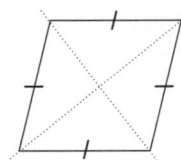

24. **E 7.1**
    The number 7.09 represents 7 ones, no tenths and 9 hundredths.
    Rounded to the nearest tenth, this is 7 ones and 1 tenth, 7.1
25. **C 285**
    399 ÷ 7 = 57 (represents $\frac{1}{7}$ of the people)
    $\frac{5}{7}$ of the people do not win a prize.
    57 × 5 = 285
26. **A (3.5, 4.5)**
    Point P is 3.5 units along and 4.5 units up.
27. **D 245**
    Total silver medals = 128
    Total bronze medals = 117
    128 + 117 = 245
28. **C 2**

29. **E Trapezium, parallelogram, square**
30. **C −6°C**
    1°C − 7°C = −6°C
31. **E 120**
    45 + 50 + 25 = 120
32. **A 10.2**
    8.5 is five-sixths
    So one-sixth is 8.5 ÷ 5 = 1.7
    1.7 × 6 = 10.2
33. **A 1200 litres**
    20 cm is a reduction of $\frac{1}{3}$ of the volume of oil $(\frac{20}{60})$.
    $\frac{1}{3}$ of 1800 litres is 600 litres.
    The amount of oil left in the cylinder is 1800 litres − 600 litres = 1200 litres.
34. **C 135°**
    Each section of the compass is $\frac{1}{8}$ of the angle round a point (360°).
    360 ÷ 8 = 45 so each section is 45°.
    From South West to North is three sections.
    3 × 45° = 135°
35. **E 25%**
    £28 − £21 = £7 reduction
    £7 as a percentage of £28 = $\frac{7}{28}$ × 100
    = $\frac{1}{4}$ × 100 = 0.25 × 100 = 25%
36. **B 7**
    1.9 litres = 1900 ml
    1900 ÷ 250 = 7 remainder 150 ml
    So Abdi can make 7 full cups of tea.
37. **D £171**
    £378 − £36 = £342
    Grace saves half of £342 = £171
38. **A 456**
    24 × 19 = 24 × 20 − 24 = 480 − 24 = 456
39. **C Wednesday**
    There were 365 days in 2003 (leap years with 366 days happen every 4 years in even years).
    Each week has 7 days and 52 weeks × 7 = 364 days.
    So if July 23rd 2002 was a Tuesday, the same date in 2003 was a Wednesday (one day after).
40. **C £8.60**
    One calculator costs £10.40 ÷ 2 = £5.20
    One pen costs £3.54 ÷ 3 = £1.18
    One calculator and one pen cost £6.38
    30 calculators and 30 pens cost
    £6.38 × 30 = £191.40
    £200 − £191.40 = £8.60
41. **B 1.96 kg**
    Each interval represents 0.02 kg (two-tenths of a kilogram).
    The arrow points to the third line on the scale, which is 1.96 kg.
42. **D 92.04**
    Multiply 708 by 13 to get 9204 then divide by 100 (as 7.08 is 100 times smaller than 708) to get 92.04
43. **D $23.40**
    On Wednesday, the exchange rate was £1 = $1.17
    £20 × 1.17 = $23.40
44. **A**
    The square-based pyramid has eight edges: four on the base and four leading up to the top vertex.

45. **E 72**
    Working backwards:
    5 (Bella's output) add 3 is equal to 8, then multiply by 9
    8 × 9 = 72 (Bella's input)
46. **A $\frac{1}{21}$**
    $\frac{2}{7} + \frac{2}{3} = \frac{6}{21} + \frac{14}{21} = \frac{20}{21}$
    $1 - \frac{20}{21} = \frac{1}{21}$ so there are $\frac{1}{21}$ socks that are neither black nor white.
47. **B 0.375**
    1 ÷ 8 = 0.125
    0.125 × 3 = 0.375
48. **E 2, 7, 13**
    182 is even and so is divisible by 2.
    182 divided by 2 is 91.
    7 multiplied by 13 is 91.
    So the three prime numbers are 2, 7 and 13.
49. **C £623.75**
    4.99 × 125 = 499 × 1.25 =
    500 × 1.25 − 1.25 = 623.75
50. **B 20.25**
    The rule for this sequence is multiply by 1.5
    4 × 1.5 = 6, 6 × 1.5 = 9, 9 × 1.5 = 13.5, 13.5 × 1.5 = 20.25

Practice Test B Answers and Explanations

1. **D 12**
   3 × 51 = 153
   153 ÷ 13 = 11 remainder 10, so 12 minibuses would be needed.
2. **A** All angles in a rhombus are always equal.
3. **D £5.39**
   £10 − £2.75 = £7.25
   62p × 3 = 186p = £1.86
   £7.25 − £1.86 = £5.39
4. **C 32**
   The sequence increases by 4.5 each time.
   Continuing the sequence gives 5, 9.5, 14, 18.5, 23, 27.5, **32**
5. **B 8**
   Dawn's brother is currently 22 − 6 = 16
   So Dawn is half of 16 = 8
6. **B $1\frac{11}{24}$**
   $5\frac{1}{3} - 3\frac{7}{8} = \frac{16}{3} - \frac{31}{8} = \frac{128}{24} - \frac{93}{24} = \frac{35}{24} = 1\frac{11}{24}$
7. **C 294°**
   There are 180° in a triangle and 360° around a point.
   The third angle in the triangle is 180° − 58° − 56° = 66°
   To work out x, 360° − 66° = 294°
8. **A 8 hours 27 minutes**
   12 minutes added to 05:48 gets to 06:00. Another 8 hours gets to 14:00 and another 15 minutes gets to 14:15, making a total of 8 hours and 27 minutes.
9. **E Friday, 12°C**
   The greatest difference is on Friday as the gap between the bars is the largest. The difference is 16°C − 4°C = 12°C
10. **E 240**
    If 20% of Alex's number is 64, then 10% is 32 and 5% is 16.
    75% is therefore 7 × 32 + 16 = 224 + 16 = 240
11. **A 49.52**
12. **D 20 cm**
    The cube has 12 edges.
    240 ÷ 12 = 20
    Each edge is 20 cm in length.
13. **C Kite**

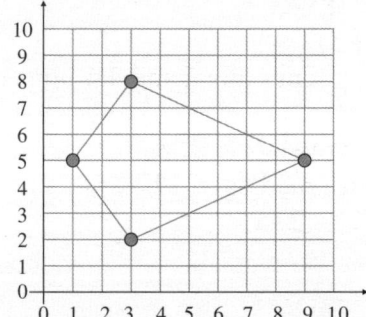

14. **B 0.73**
    The largest decimal in the list is 0.9
    The smallest decimal is 0.17
    0.90 − 0.17 = 0.73
15. **B 1**
    $0.75 = \frac{3}{4}$ so, $0.75 \div \frac{3}{4} = \frac{3}{4} \div \frac{3}{4}$ or 0.75 ÷ 0.75 = 1
16. **E 2750 g**
    There are 1000 grams in a kilogram.
    2.75 × 1000 = 2750
17. **D £2.80**
    £630 ÷ 45 = £14
    £14 ÷ 5 = £2.80
18. **E −10**
    −10 + 7 = −3

19. **A 10**
Each small square on the horizontal axis of the graph represents 5 minutes.
Amy stops twice for 5 minutes each time, so her total stopping time is 10 minutes.

20. **B 2**
Each row, column and diagonal totals 18 (3 + 8 + 7).

5	10	3
4	6	8
9	2	7

21. **C 64%**
The total number of teachers is
16 + 6 + 3 = 25
16 teachers walk to school, which can be written as $\frac{16}{25} = \frac{64}{100} = 64\%$

22. **C 28**
If Tina is x years old, Auntie Flo is $2x$ years old and Grandma is $6x$ years old.
Together, $x + 2x + 6x = 9x = 126$ years
$126 \div 9 = 14$
So Tina is 14 and Auntie Flo is 28.

23. **A £24**
The difference between the prices paid is 5% (15% − 10%).
5% = £1.20 and so 100% (full price) = £1.20 × 20 = £24

24. **D 1 + 2 × 3 × 4**
A: 1 × 2 + 3 + 4 = 9
B: 1 + 2 × 3 + 4 = 11
C: 1 × 2 + 3 × 4 = 14
D: 1 + 2 × 3 × 4 = 25
and 25 is a multiple of 5
E: 1 × 2 × 3 × 4 = 24

25. **B P and T**
The two shapes with line symmetry are P and T.

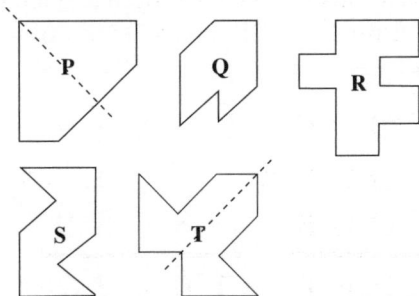

26. **E 17**
In the Venn diagram, the overlap between chocolate and strawberry is 10, so 10 children liked both chocolate and strawberry. You must also include the 7 children who liked chocolate, strawberry and vanilla. 10 + 7 = 17

27. **C HL**
Side AB will meet side HL when folded.

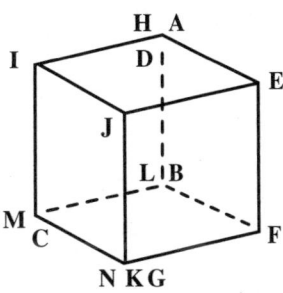

28. **E 56 cm**
Missing side is
5 cm + 3 cm + 5 cm = 13 cm
13 cm + 3 cm + 5 cm + 12 cm + 3 cm + 12 cm + 5 cm + 3 cm = 56 cm

29. **B 350 ml**
There is 150 ml of undiluted squash in the jug.
0.5 litres = 500 ml
500 ml − 150 ml = 350 ml of water needs to be added to make 0.5 litres.

30. **E 19**
Annie can buy six lots of three sweets for 30p each. This will cost 6 × 30p = 180p (£1.80). She can then buy one more sweet costing 12p, making a total of 19 sweets.

31. **C 1820 cm³**
20 cm × 7 cm = 140 cm² (area of base)
140 cm² × 13 cm = 1820 cm³

32. **E 235**
9.23 a.m. plus 4 hours is 1.23 p.m.
4 hours is 240 minutes (4 × 60)
1.23 p.m. − 5 minutes = 1.18 p.m.
So the total number of minutes between the two times is 240 − 5 = 235

33. **A $\frac{2}{3}$**
A regular hexagon is made up of six equilateral triangles.
Two full triangles and four half triangles are shaded, which equals $\frac{4}{6} \left(= \frac{2}{3}\right)$ of the hexagon.

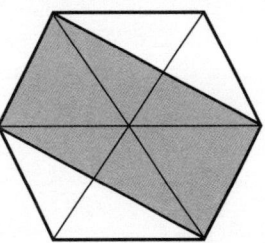

34. **B 1**
The sequence decreases by $\frac{3}{4}$ each time.
$1\frac{3}{4} - \frac{3}{4} = 1$

35. **C 500 g**
Each cake needs 225 ÷ 9 = 25 g of flour.
20 × 25 g = 500 g needed for 20 cakes.

36. **B 21**
The proportion of children that chose apple is a little over a quarter.
$\frac{1}{4}$ of 72 = 18 and so answer B, 21, would be the best estimate.

37. **E £6.04**
7 biscuits cost 7 × 72p = 504p = £5.04
4 sandwiches cost 4 × £2.23 = £8.92
Total cost is £5.04 + £8.92 = £13.96
The change should be
£20 − £13.96 = £6.04

38. **D 700 ml**
Each interval on the scale is 200 ml.
There is 1300 ml in the container.
Adding another 700 ml will make 2 litres.

39. **D 36 800 m**
1000 m = 1 km
36.78 km = 36 780 m
To the nearest 100 metres,
36 780 = 36 800 m

40. **C 11**
Add or subtract to fill in all the squares until the value for * is found.

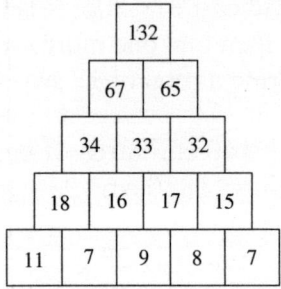

41. **B**
The reflected image is B. It can help to turn your paper so that the mirror line is vertical.

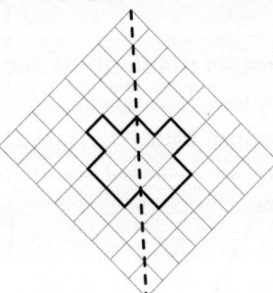

42. **E $\frac{3}{8}$**
$\frac{1}{2}$ is less than $\frac{4}{7}$ $\left(\frac{7}{14} < \frac{8}{14}\right)$
$\frac{1}{2}$ is less than $\frac{5}{9}$ $\left(\frac{9}{18} < \frac{10}{18}\right)$
$\frac{1}{2}$ is less than $\frac{3}{5}$ $\left(\frac{5}{10} < \frac{6}{10}\right)$
And $\frac{3}{8}$ is less than $\frac{1}{2}$ $\left(\frac{3}{8} < \frac{4}{8}\right)$ and so $\frac{3}{8}$ is the smallest fraction in the list.

43. **B 1**
Start by working out 3 + 3 (inside the brackets) and then divide by 3.
3 + 3 = 6, then 6 ÷ 3 = 2 and 3 − 2 = 1

44. **D Tuesday and Friday**
Total time in minutes for
Monday = 19 + 23 + 13 + 17 = 72
Tuesday = 17 + 26 + 14 + 20 = 77
Wednesday = 21 + 19 + 11 + 16 = 67
Thursday = 23 + 22 + 12 + 18 = 75
Friday = 17 + 24 + 15 + 21 = 77
The children took the same amount of time (77 minutes) on Tuesday and Friday.

45. **E 25°**
There are 180° on a straight line and so the interior angle of the triangle next to 55° = 180° − 55° = 125°
The interior angle next to
150° = 180° − 150° = 30°
There are 180° in a triangle so
angle x = 180° − 125° − 30° = 25°

46. **A 750**
50 squared = 50 × 50 = 2500
10% of 2500 = 250
30% of 2500 = 250 × 3 = 750

47. **C 225 cm²**
The perimeter of the rectangle is 40 cm + 70 cm + 40 cm + 70 cm = 220 cm
Each side of the square is
220 cm ÷ 4 = 55 cm
The area of the square
= 55 cm × 55 cm = 3025 cm²
The area of the rectangle
= 40 cm × 70 cm = 2800 cm²
The difference between the areas
= 3025 cm² − 2800 cm² = 225 cm²

48. **E 1986**
2003 − 17 = 1986

49. **C 14 000 mm**
A typical bus is about 14 metres in length.
14 000 mm = 1400 cm = 14 metres

50. **B 0**

```
  F O U R        3 6 5 9
  F O U R +      3 6 5 9 +
  F O U R        3 6 5 9
  ―――――――       ―――――――
  T H R E E      1 0 9 7 7
```

The letter H is zero.

Practice Test C Answers and Explanations

1. **D 58°**
   There are 180° in a triangle.
   180° − 59° − 63° = 58°
2. **A 109**
   5770 ÷ 53 = 108 remainder 46
   So 109 buses are needed.
3. **D X and Y**

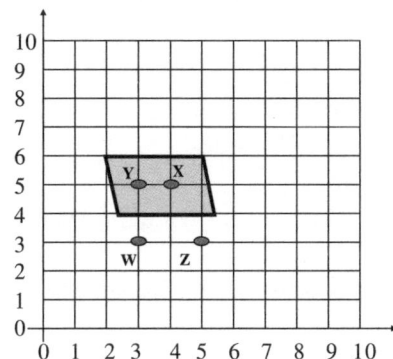

4. **C 550**
   66 ÷ 12 = 5.5
   66 ÷ 0.12 is 100 times larger (550)
5. **E 12**
   $\frac{4}{7}$ of 63 = 63 ÷ 7 × 4 = 9 × 4 = 36
   $\frac{1}{3}$ of 36 = 36 ÷ 3 = 12
6. **E $\frac{29}{120}$**
   All of the fractions are $\frac{1}{n}$ away from $\frac{1}{4}$ (where n is the denominator in each of the fractions in the question).
   $\frac{10}{40} = \frac{1}{4}, \frac{15}{60} = \frac{1}{4}, \frac{20}{80} = \frac{1}{4}, \frac{25}{100} = \frac{1}{4}, \frac{30}{120} = \frac{1}{4}$
   Since $\frac{1}{120}$ is the smallest unit fraction, then $\frac{29}{120}$ is the closest fraction to $\frac{1}{4}$
7. **D 50 cm**
   The perimeter = 8 cm + 8 cm + 10 cm + 3 cm + 7 cm + 14 cm = 50 cm
8. **A £90**
   $\frac{5}{12}$ of 360 = 360 ÷ 12 × 5 = 30 × 5
   = £150 given to her brother.
   $\frac{1}{3}$ of 360 = 360 ÷ 3 = £120 given to her sister.
   £360 − £150 − £120 = £90 left
9. **A 72**
   Multiples of 8 between 60 and 80 are 64, 72 and 80.
   72 is the only one of these that is a multiple of 3.
10. **E −46**
    The sequence subtracts 3 to get the next term.
    −13, −16, −19, −22, −25, −28, −31, −34, −37, −40, −43, **−46**
    The only number listed in the answers that will be in the sequence is −46
11. **B £276**
    10% of 240 = 24 and so 15% of 240 is 24 + 12 = 36
    The cost of the bike this year is £240 + £36 = £276
12. **D 14**
    Each square on the scale of the bar chart represents 2 people.
    17 people chose football and 3 people chose tennis as their favourite sport.
    17 − 3 = 14
13. **C 34**
    1.72 metres = 172 cm
    172 ÷ 5 = 34 (remainder 2)
14. **B £430**
    If one hen and four lambs cost £190 then two hens and eight lambs would cost £380 (double).
    Subtracting two hens and three lambs (costing £180) from two hens and eight lambs costing £380 leaves five lambs costing £200.
    One lamb costs £200 ÷ 5 = £40
    If one lamb costs £40 then two hens plus (3 × £40) £120 equals £180
    This means that two hens cost £180 − £120 = £60 and so one hen costs £30
    Five hens and seven lambs cost (5 × £30 + 7 × £40) = £430
15. **E 91 cm²**
    If the perimeter of the rectangle is 40 cm, the width plus the length must equal half of 40, i.e. 20 cm.
    6 + w + w = 20 so w = 7
    The length of the rectangle is 6 + 7 = 13 cm and the width is 7 cm.
    So the area is 13 cm × 7 cm = 91 cm²
16. **C 10.15**
    Each small gap on the number line represents one-tenth.
    The arrow points in-between 10.1 and 10.2, so 10.15
17. **D 13**
    Working backwards:
    38 + 1 = 39
    39 ÷ 3 = 13
18. **D 40**
    Each coin is 25 mm in diameter, which is 2.5 cm (10 mm = 1 cm).
    1 metre = 100 cm
    100 ÷ 2.5 = 40

19. B $\frac{11}{12}$
£6 = 600p, and there is 50p change so he spent £5.50 = 550p
The fraction is $\frac{550}{600} = \frac{11}{12}$

20. A 1.282
65% = 0.65 as a decimal
$\frac{1}{8} = 0.125$
Adding all the numbers gives
0.507 + 0.65 + 0.125 = 1.282

21. C
Comparing the unit prices (dividing cost by number of cakes):
A = 55p, B = 50p, C = 45p, D = 53p and E = 51.25p
So stall C is the best value for money.

22. C 3
Working backwards:
30 − 6 = 24
24 ÷ 2 = 12 (second term)
12 − 6 = 6
6 ÷ 2 = 3

23. A 17 467

24. E 35
£30 = 3000p
3000 ÷ 85 = 35 remainder 25, so Molly can buy 35 plants

25. D 28
The bottom layer of the shape is made up of an odd number of cubes in a cross shape. In the fourth shape there will be a bottom layer of cubes with 13 cubes like this:

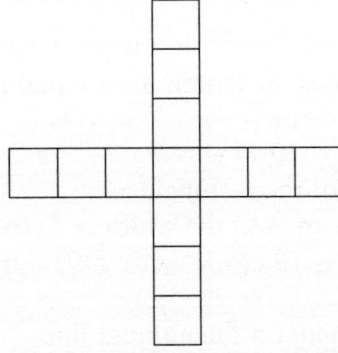

The third shape has 15 cubes (6 + 9) and so the fourth shape will have
15 + 13 = 28 cubes.
Another way to work this out is to notice that the sequence goes 1, 6, 15 so the difference is increasing by 4 each time. The next difference will be (9 + 4 = 13) and 15 + 13 = 28

26. E 5
Four out of the 12 hexagons are shaded in the diagram.
$\frac{3}{4}$ of 12 = 9 so 5 more hexagons need to be shaded (4 + 5 = 9)

27. A 1.13 m
96 cm + 17 cm = 113 cm = 1.13 m

28. B Billie
Asif scored 77 + 76 + 80 = 233
Billie scored 67 + 74 + 60 = 201
Cara scored 81 + 84 + 88 = 253
Deepak scored 60 + 82 + 68 = 210
Ellie scored 80 + 78 + 64 = 222

29. E 240
£6.90 minus the 90p for the cover leaves £6 for the pages.
£6 = 600p
Each page costs 2.5p
600 ÷ 2.5 = 240 pages

30. D 8.19 a.m.
7.37 a.m. add 14 minutes gets Amy to the shop at 7.51 a.m.
She spends 5 minutes in the shop, so leaves the shop at 7.56 a.m.
She arrives at school 23 minutes later, which is 8.19 a.m.

31. B 9

32. D 4

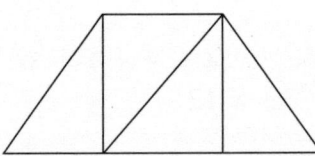

33. E 8
200 ÷ 8 = 16 remainder 8

34. D 135
There are 12 months in a year.
11 × 12 = 132
One quarter of a year = 3 months
132 + 3 = 135

35. B 98 cm²
If the wire is 42 cm long, this is the perimeter of the rectangle.
Length + width = perimeter ÷ 2, so the length + the width = 21 cm
The length is twice the width, so the width must be 7 cm (21 ÷ 3)
The length is 14 cm (7 × 2)
The area of the rectangle will be
14 cm × 7 cm = 98 cm²

36. A 25
As the graph is a straight line and passes through (0, 0), the points are in proportion.
2 × 5 = 10 and so 5 × 5 = 25
The coordinates of y are (10, 25).

37. D 49 917
50 017 − 100 = 49 917

38. **E 64**
    If 25% of * is 16, then 16 must be 25% of *.
    25% = $\frac{1}{4}$
    $\frac{1}{4}$ of 64 = 16   (64 = 16 × 4)
39. **A 9 cm²**
    A cube has six faces.
    54 ÷ 6 = 9
    Each face has an area of 9 cm².
40. **C 24°**
    The base angles of an isosceles triangle are equal.
    The base angles of the triangle are both
    180° − 102° = 78°
    78° + 78° = 156°
    There are 180° in a triangle so
    angle x = 180° − 156° = 24°
41. **E 36**
    25% is 24 games and so 100% is
    24 × 4 = 96 games played in total.
    96 − 24 = 72 games were either won or lost.
    These were equal so the team won
    72 ÷ 2 = 36 games
42. **C 13**

	Red	Blue	Total
Squares	6	11	17
Circles	8	5	13
Total	14	16	30

43. **B 7.48 a.m.**
    There are 25 minutes from 8 a.m. until 8.25 a.m.
    37 − 25 = 12
    12 minutes before 8 a.m. is 7.48 a.m.
44. **A 39p**
    £3.90 = 390p
    390 ÷ 15 = 26 so Rosie paid 26p per bar.
    A profit of 50% would add on 13p to each bar (13 is 50% of 26 or 26 ÷ 2 = 13)
    Rosie would need to sell each bar for
    26 + 13 = 39p
    Or 50% of 390p is $\frac{390}{2}$ = 195
    195 + 390 = 585
    $\frac{585}{15}$ = 39p
45. **C Letter L**
    Only the letter L does not have line symmetry.

     L T

46. **D 110 cm²**
    The two missing lengths are shown below.
    18 cm − 13 cm = 5 cm, making the length of the smaller rectangle
    6 + 5 = 11 cm
    15 cm − 12 cm = 3 cm, making the width of the rectangle 7 cm + 3 cm = 10 cm
    The area of the smaller rectangle is
    11 × 10 = 110 cm²

    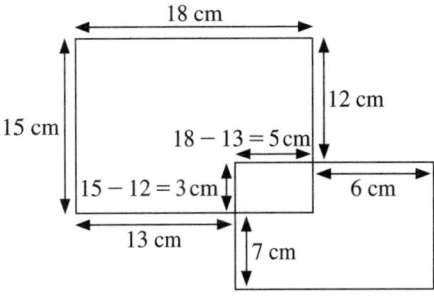

47. **A South**
    A 270° turn is three-quarters of a complete turn (three right angles).
    Anticlockwise travels the opposite way to a clock (to the left).
    Three-quarters of a turn from East going anticlockwise arrives at South.
48. **E 8**
    There are four right angles in a complete turn (90° × 4 = 360°).
    So there are eight right angles in two complete turns.
49. **E 36**
    Eva eats one-half.
    Two-thirds of one-half is one-third (or two-sixths) so Mo eats one-third.
    One-half plus one-third is five-sixths, leaving one-sixth (Charlie's share).
    6 sweets is one-sixth and so multiplying by 6 gives the total number of sweets, 36.
50. **B 11**
    Jack and Freddie's ages add to 32 and Jack is two years younger than Freddie.
    32 − 2 = 30
    30 ÷ 2 = 15, so Jack is 15
    And Freddie is 15 + 2 = 17
    Orla is six years younger than Freddie, so she is 17 − 6 = 11

Practice Test D Answers and Explanations

1. **C** 7 065 028
2. **E** 165°
   As there are 12 hours around the clock, each hour is 360° ÷ 12 = 30°
   Between the hands at 12.30, there are five-and-a-half hours.
   5.5 × 30° = 165° or 180° − 15° = 165°
3. **B** 200 miles
   To convert 320 km into miles, divide by 8 and multiply by 5 (every 8 km = 5 miles).
   320 ÷ 8 × 5 = 200 miles
4. **A** £100.60
   £10.06 × 10 = £100.60
5. **D** −7
   $(-3)^2 = -3 \times -3 = 9$
   −16 + 9 = 9 − 16 = −7
6. **B** 55
   19 × 3 = 57
   57 − 2 = 55
7. **D** 15%
   By rounding both numbers, you can estimate the percentage of the UK population in London.
   69 140 000 can be rounded to 70 000 000 and 9 650 000 can be rounded to 10 000 000.
   10 000 000 ÷ 70 000 000 = 1 ÷ 7 = 0.14... which is about 15%.
8. **A** 8
   Minah gave away two-thirds of her sweets (leaving one-third).
   Eight-twelfths is the same as two-thirds, $\frac{2}{3} = \frac{8}{12}$
   If each of Minah's friends received one-twelfth, then Minah shared her sweets with eight friends.
9. **E** 2240 cm²
   Each rectangle has an area of 35 cm × 8 cm = 280 cm²
   There are eight sides,
   so 280 cm² × 8 = 2240 cm²
10. **C** 2.95 and 3.05
    If the puppy has a mass of 3 kg to the nearest 100 g, it is between 2.95 kg (50 g less than 3 kg) and 3.05 kg (50 g more than 3 kg).
11. **C** 539
    The lowest possible sum of the two given numbers is 775 + 125 = 900
    The greatest possible sum of the two given numbers is 825 + 175 = 1000
    This means that the remaining number must be between 500 and 600 (to add to 1500).
    The only number in the answer options between 500 and 600 is 539.
12. **A** 0.85
    51 ÷ 6 = 8.5
    $\frac{51}{60} = \frac{8.5}{10} = 0.85$
13. **D** 33 km
    Every 1 cm on the map represents 6 km in real life.
    The towns are 5.5 cm apart on the map, which is 5.5 × 6 = 33 km in real life.
14. **B** 64
    There are two girls for every boy, so divide 96 into three parts.
    96 ÷ 3 = 32
    Two parts are girls.
    32 × 2 = 64
15. **C** 125 g
    The table gives values per 100 g.
    There are 1000 g in 1 kg so the values in the table need to be multiplied by 10 (100 × 10 = 1000) to give equivalent values for 1000 g.
    12.50 × 10 = 125 g
16. **A** 2.98 g
    Each step on the scale represents 0.02 g as there are five steps between each tenth of a gram separated by lines on the diagram.
    The arrow points to the fourth line after 2.9 g, which is 2.98 g.
17. **B** Shape W

    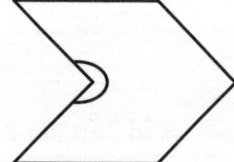

    Shape W is the only shape with a reflex angle (greater than 180°).
18. **B** 3
    Lena has 10 bananas, which can make 6 smoothies ($1\frac{1}{2} \times 6 = 9$)
    She has 15 strawberries which can make 3 smoothies (4 × 3 = 12)
    She has 22 blueberries, which can make 4 smoothies (5 × 4 = 20)
    Lena can make 3 smoothies (as she will then run out of strawberries).
19. **E** 7
    There is one extra can in every row.
    1 + 2 + 3 + 4 + 5 + 6 + 7 = 28

20. **D** $\frac{3}{11}$

There are 44 children altogether (the sum of all the numbers in the Venn diagram, including the 4 children who hadn't visited any of the countries.)
12 children visited both France and Spain (9 visited only France and Spain and 3 visited France, Spain and Germany).
$\frac{12}{44} = \frac{3}{11}$

21. **A** 27

In the large cube, there are 3 layers each with nine 1 cm cubes.
$3 \times 9 = 27$ cubes

22. **C** £8.32

$8 \times £1.46 = £11.68$
$£20.00 - £11.68 = £8.32$

23. **E** 66°

There are 180° on a straight line,
$180° - 124° = 56°$
There are 180° in a triangle,
$180° - 56° - 58° = 66°$

24. **E** 21

Football (F)   Swimming (S)
Hockey (H)   Netball (N)
Basketball (B)   Golf (G)
The possible combinations are:
FF, FS, FH, FN, FB, FG (6)
SS, SH, SN, SB, SG (5)
HH, HN, HB, HG (4)
NN, NB, NG (3)
BB, BG (2)
GG (1)
(FS is the same two sports as SF so is not repeated.)
$6 + 5 + 4 + 3 + 2 + 1 = 21$

25. **A** Chris

Chris's maths score was 9, which was the highest.

26. **E** **There are two more cats than dogs in the rescue centre.**

As there are an odd number of cats and dogs, there must be an odd number of cats and an even number of dogs or an even number of cats and an odd number of dogs. This means there could be more cats or more dogs and the difference can be any odd number up to 37 (e.g. 38 cats and 1 dog). E is not correct as the difference cannot be even (as this would make the total even).

27. **D**

28. **B** $\frac{5}{9}$

The order of the fractions from smallest to largest is: $\frac{1}{4}, \frac{3}{7}, \frac{5}{9}, \frac{7}{8}, \frac{15}{16}$

29. **C** 5

Going backwards through the number machine gives:
$7 \times 4 = 28$
$28 + 7 = 35$
$35 \div 7 = 5$

30. **E** 4

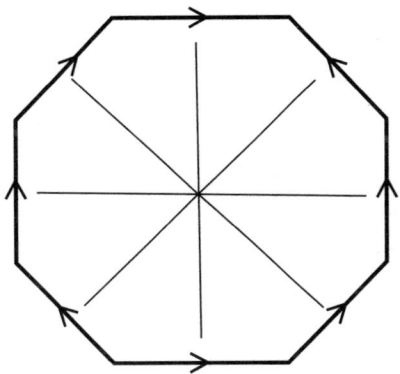

There are four pairs of parallel lines in a regular octagon (opposite sides).

31. **B** 82 km/h

The arrow is pointing to 72 km/h.
If the car speeds up by 10 km/h, it will be travelling at 82 km/h.

32. **C** £17.50

The area of the garden to be covered is $6.5 \times 4 = 26$ square metres.
Each bag of fertiliser covers 6 square metres.
To find out how many bags are needed, divide 26 by 6. This gives 4 and a third $\left(\frac{26}{6} = \frac{13}{3} = 4\frac{1}{3}\right)$.
To cover the garden, 5 bags of fertiliser are needed (4 won't be enough).
$5 \times £3.50 = £17.50$

33. **D** £24.25

$97 \times 25 = 2425p$ or £24.25

34. **B** 7

The sequence goes $2\frac{1}{3}, 4\frac{2}{3}, 7, 9\frac{1}{3}, 11\frac{2}{3}…$
The number 7 is in the sequence.

35. **A** 8

A vertex is where two or more edges of a 3D shape meet (the corners).

36. **E** 8

$27 - (1 + 3 + 4 + 6 + 5) = 27 - 19 = 8$

37. **D** 5 minutes and 47 seconds

Kate took 6 minutes and 23 seconds to complete the puzzle.
Jenny took 2 minutes and 40 seconds longer, which is 9 minutes and 3 seconds.
Alex took 3 minutes and 16 seconds less than Jenny, which is 5 minutes and 47 seconds.

38. **C 46**
The number of children represented for each size is size 1 = 7, size 2 = 14, size 3 = 15, size 4 = 7 and size 5 = 3
7 + 14 + 15 + 7 + 3 = 46

39. **E 23 × 24 + 26 − 27**
The multiplication is done first (order of operations) and then the addition and subtraction.
The smallest product is 23 × 24 = 552, then 26 − 27 gives −1, giving a total of 551.
This is the smallest answer.

40. **B 1.73**
$\frac{3}{4} = 0.75$
$\frac{39}{50} = \frac{78}{100} = 0.78$
0.75 + 0.2 + 0.78 = 1.73

41. **A (7, 2) (9, 2) (8, 5)**

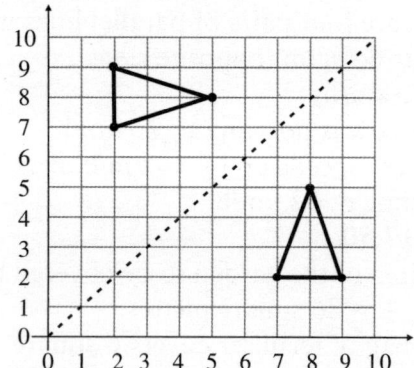

42. **C 127°**
There are 360° in a quadrilateral.
The shape has two right angles
(90° + 90° = 180°)
360° − 180° − 53° = 127°

43. **A 100 cm²**
The dimensions of the shaded square are
15 cm − 5 cm = 10 cm by
15 cm − 5 cm = 10 cm.
The area is 10 cm × 10 cm = 100 cm²

44. **E 16 km**
One mile = $\frac{8}{5}$ kilometres
so 10 miles = $10 \times \frac{8}{5} = \frac{80}{5} = 16$ km

45. **E 28**
The first four prime numbers are 2, 3, 5 and 7. They sum to 17.
The next prime number is 11.
17 + 11 = 28

46. **C £6.42**
The five pens cost £20 − £9.30 = £10.70
One pen costs £10.70 ÷ 5 = £2.14
Three pens cost £2.14 × 3 = £6.42

47. **B 36 cm²**
If the perimeter of the rectangle is 32 cm, the sum of the length and the width must be 32 cm ÷ 2 = 16 cm
The area of the rectangle is the length multiplied by the width. These two numbers must sum to 16.
There are no two numbers that sum to 16 and have a product of 36.

48. **A**

49. **C 15% of 360**
A, B, D and E are all equal to 48
15% of 360 = 54

50. **D 38**
On the last day, Jacob ate the number of blueberries that he ate on the first day plus 32 (4 × 8).
An equation can be formed to find the number of blueberries he ate on the first day.
Let X be the number he ate on the first day.

Day	1	2	3	4	5
Blueberries	X	X + 8	X + 16	X + 24	X + 32

5X + 80 = 110
 5X = 30
  X = 6
On the last day Jacob ate 6 + 32 = 38 blueberries.

MATHEMATICS TEST A

MA A

Pupil's Name

School Name

Date of Test

DATE OF BIRTH

Please mark like this ⊣.

1
- 20 401
- 204 010
- 204 100
- 20 410
- 240 010

2
- 20 753
- 53 130
- 61 743
- 61 753
- 43 753

3
- 30°
- 45°
- 120°
- 90°
- 60°

4
- £17.49
- £23.30
- £22.67
- £17.82
- £17.00

5
- A
- B
- C
- D
- E

6
- 121
- 1331
- 1111
- 11
- 14 641

7
- 318 m
- 310 m
- 155 m
- 159 m
- 314 m

8
- 9
- 18
- 19
- 20
- 17

9
- 3
- 4
- 5
- 6
- 7

10
- Trapezium
- Pentagon
- Parallelogram
- Hexagon
- Octagon

11
- 4
- 5
- 6
- 7
- 8

12
- £13.44
- £14.93
- £5.48
- £8.40
- £6.40

13
- A
- B
- C
- D
- E

14
- 143
- 390
- 1300
- 338
- 1100

15
- 55.964
- 52.994
- 19.001
- 52.301
- 52.4

16
- 4
- 5
- 6
- 7
- 8

17
- £60.55
- £86.50
- £65.50
- £25.95
- £6.50

18
- 35
- 40
- 45
- 50
- 55

19
- 112 cm²
- 224 cm²
- 96 cm²
- 152 cm²
- 560 cm²

20
- 30°
- 45°
- 90°
- 120°
- 60°

21
- 220 g
- 165 g
- 240 g
- 360 g
- 118 g

22
- 2
- 3
- 4
- 5
- 6

23
- 6
- 9
- 4
- 3
- 7

24
- 8.0
- 7.9
- 7.01
- 8.9
- 7.1

© HarperCollins*Publishers* Ltd

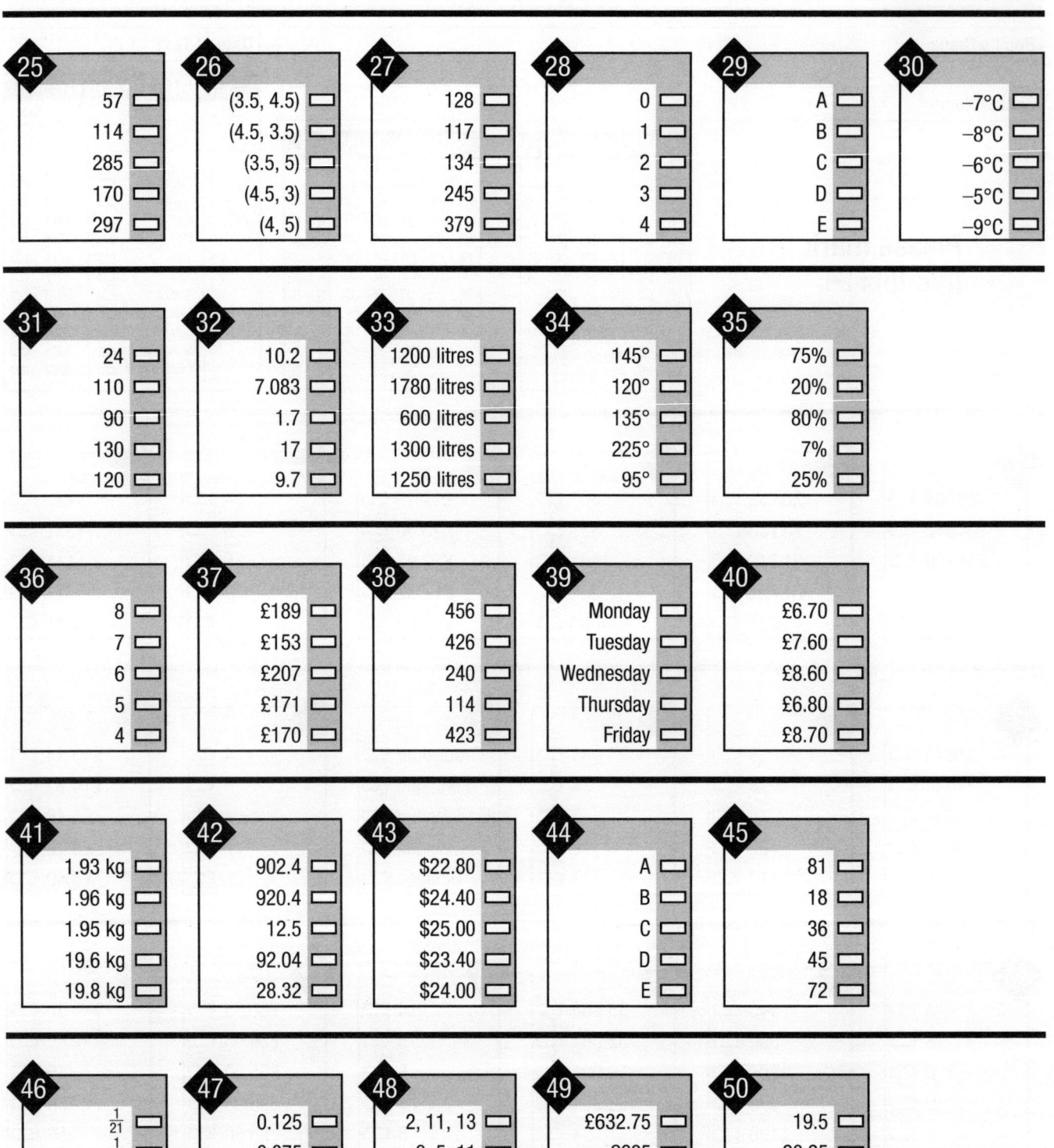

MATHEMATICS TEST B

MA B

Pupil's Name

School Name

Date of Test

DATE OF BIRTH

Day	Month	Year
[0] [0]	January ☐	2011 ☐
[1] [1]	February ☐	2012 ☐
[2] [2]	March ☐	2013 ☐
[3] [3]	April ☐	2014 ☐
[4]	May ☐	2015 ☐
[5]	June ☐	2016 ☐
[6]	July ☐	2017 ☐
[7]	August ☐	2018 ☐
[8]	September ☐	2019 ☐
[9]	October ☐	2020 ☐
	November ☐	2021 ☐
	December ☐	2022 ☐

PUPIL NUMBER / **SCHOOL NUMBER**: grids [0]–[9]

Please mark like this ⊢.

1. 9 ☐ 10 ☐ 11 ☐ 12 ☐ 13 ☐

2. A ☐ B ☐ C ☐ D ☐ E ☐

3. £6.63 ☐ £6.01 ☐ £2.64 ☐ £5.39 ☐ £4.39 ☐

4. 27.5 ☐ 18.5 ☐ 32 ☐ 23 ☐ 32.5 ☐

5. 16 ☐ 8 ☐ 11 ☐ 19 ☐ 12 ☐

6. $2\frac{11}{24}$ ☐ $1\frac{11}{24}$ ☐ $2\frac{13}{24}$ ☐ $1\frac{13}{24}$ ☐ $\frac{11}{24}$ ☐

7. 66° ☐ 302° ☐ 294° ☐ 114° ☐ 304° ☐

8. A ☐ B ☐ C ☐ D ☐ E ☐

9. A ☐ B ☐ C ☐ D ☐ E ☐

10. 640 ☐ 256 ☐ 320 ☐ 204 ☐ 240 ☐

11. 49.52 ☐ 52.49 ☐ 45.29 ☐ 49.25 ☐ 52.94 ☐

12. 24 cm ☐ 12 cm ☐ 48 cm ☐ 20 cm ☐ 40 cm ☐

13. Parallelogram ☐ Rectangle ☐ Kite ☐ Rhombus ☐ Trapezium ☐

14. 0.77 ☐ 0.73 ☐ 0.69 ☐ 0.64 ☐ 0.56 ☐

15. $\frac{3}{4}$ ☐ 1 ☐ $\frac{1}{3}$ ☐ $\frac{1}{4}$ ☐ $\frac{4}{3}$ ☐

16. 275 g ☐ 27.5 g ☐ 27 500 g ☐ 275 000 g ☐ 2750 g ☐

17. £14 ☐ £2.60 ☐ £1.40 ☐ £2.80 ☐ £3.60 ☐

18. 4 ☐ −4 ☐ 10 ☐ 3 ☐ −10 ☐

19. 10 ☐ 5 ☐ 20 ☐ 1 ☐ 2 ☐

20. 10 ☐ 2 ☐ 5 ☐ 6 ☐ 9 ☐

21. 16% ☐ 32% ☐ 64% ☐ 60% ☐ 75% ☐

22. 84 ☐ 14 ☐ 28 ☐ 18 ☐ 24 ☐

23. £24 ☐ £12 ☐ £20 ☐ £15 ☐ £30 ☐

24. A ☐ B ☐ C ☐ D ☐ E ☐

© HarperCollinsPublishers Ltd

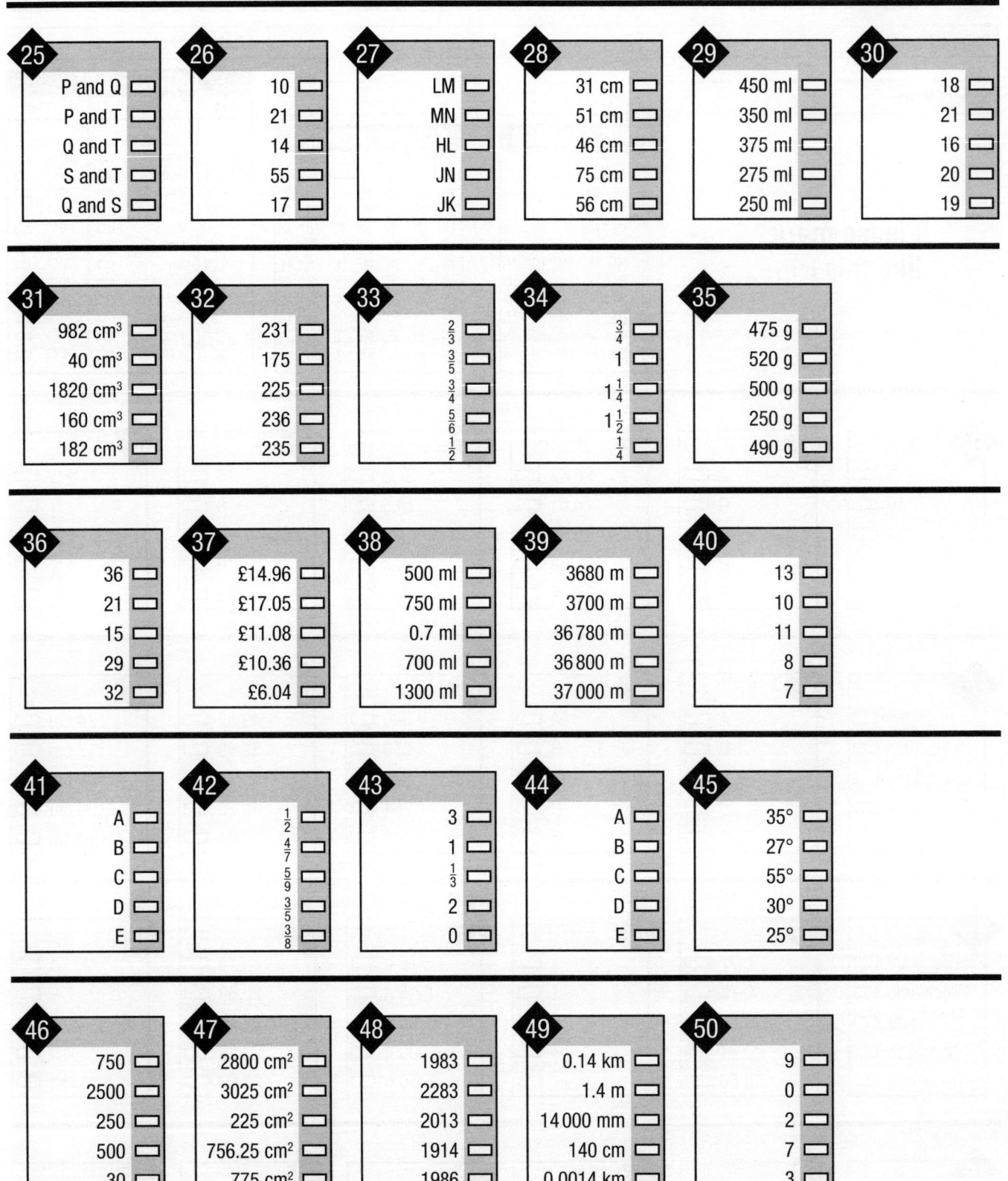

MATHEMATICS TEST C

Pupil's Name

School Name

Date of Test

DATE OF BIRTH

Please mark like this ⊢.

1
- 48°
- 63°
- 59°
- 58°
- 238°

2
- 109
- 100
- 110
- 107
- 108

3
- X, Y and Z
- X and Z
- Y and Z
- X and Y
- W, X and Y

4
- 0.55
- 5.5
- 550
- 5500
- 55

5
- 4.5
- 36
- 21
- 3
- 12

6
- $\frac{11}{40}$
- $\frac{16}{60}$
- $\frac{19}{80}$
- $\frac{26}{100}$
- $\frac{29}{120}$

7
- 44 cm
- 36 cm
- 28 cm
- 50 cm
- 56 cm

8
- £90
- £120
- £150
- £210
- £80

9
- 72
- 63
- 64
- 80
- 78

10
- −35
- −29
- −41
- −33
- −46

11
- £204
- £276
- £264
- £255
- £286

12
- 13
- 12
- 17
- 14
- 10

13
- 32
- 33
- 34
- 35
- 36

14
- £480
- £430
- £360
- £410
- £370

15
- 36 cm²
- 72 cm²
- 60 cm²
- 240 cm²
- 91 cm²

16
- 10.1
- 10.2
- 10.15
- 10.05
- 10.5

17
- 113
- 7
- 9
- 13
- 23

18
- 4
- 400
- 50
- 40
- 225

19
- $\frac{1}{12}$
- $\frac{11}{12}$
- $\frac{50}{600}$
- $\frac{45}{50}$
- $\frac{7}{12}$

20
- 1.282
- 65.632
- 1.407
- 1.957
- 1.237

21
- A
- B
- C
- D
- E

22
- 1
- 2
- 3
- 4
- 5

23
- 17 467
- 17 599
- 17 439
- 18 500
- 17 550

24
- 32
- 27
- 33
- 40
- 35

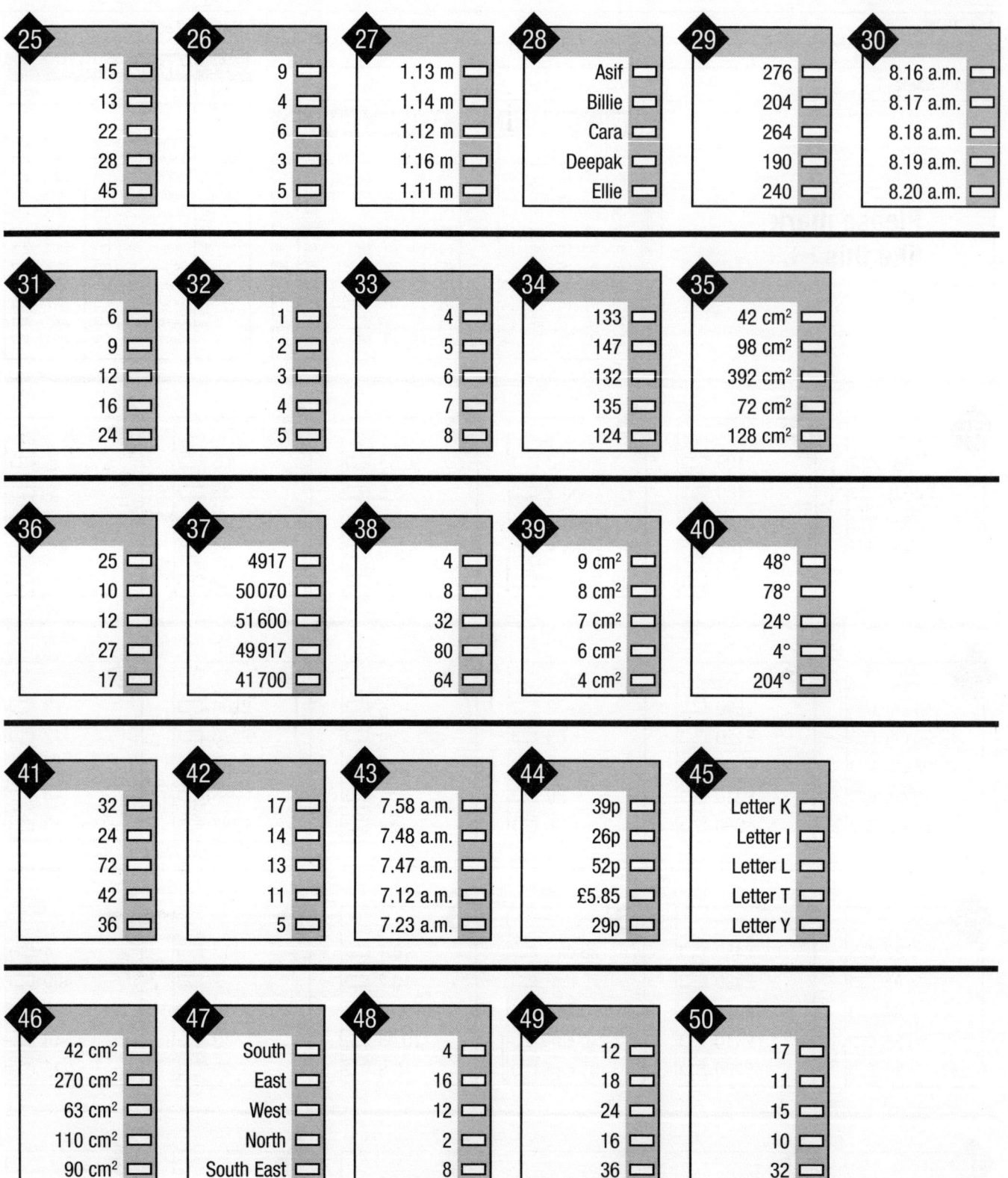

MATHEMATICS TEST D

Pupil's Name

School Name

Date of Test

DATE OF BIRTH

Please mark like this ⊟.

1
- 7 650 028
- 7 065 280
- 7 065 028
- 7 650 280
- 7 006 528

2
- 195°
- 25°
- 170°
- 150°
- 165°

3
- 512 miles
- 200 miles
- 40 miles
- 400 miles
- 220 miles

4
- £100.60
- £106.00
- £1006.00
- £10 060
- £160.00

5
- −25
- −19
- −13
- −7
- 7

6
- 48
- 55
- 36
- 57
- 45

7
- 10%
- 20%
- 5%
- 15%
- 7%

8
- 8
- 12
- 9
- 6
- 4

9
- 2420 cm^2
- 280 cm^2
- 1680 cm^2
- 17 920 cm^2
- 2240 cm^2

10
- A
- B
- C
- D
- E

11
- 418
- 683
- 539
- 752
- 338

12
- 0.85
- 0.8
- 0.51
- 0.6
- 0.75

13
- 5.5 km
- 55 km
- 27.5 km
- 33 km
- 30 km

14
- 32
- 64
- 48
- 24
- 60

15
- 1250 g
- 1.25 g
- 125 g
- 0.125 g
- 25 g

16
- 2.98 g
- 2.99 g
- 2.4 g
- 2.13 g
- 2.95 g

17
- Shape V
- Shape W
- Shape X
- Shape Y
- Shape Z

18
- 4
- 3
- 6
- 5
- 7

19
- 6
- 8
- 5
- 9
- 7

20
- $\frac{9}{40}$
- $\frac{9}{44}$
- $\frac{1}{4}$
- $\frac{3}{11}$
- $\frac{1}{3}$

21
- 27
- 9
- 81
- 54
- 18

22
- £11.24
- £11.68
- £8.32
- £9.42
- £8.42

23
- 58°
- 56°
- 76°
- 68°
- 66°

24
- 30
- 24
- 15
- 36
- 21

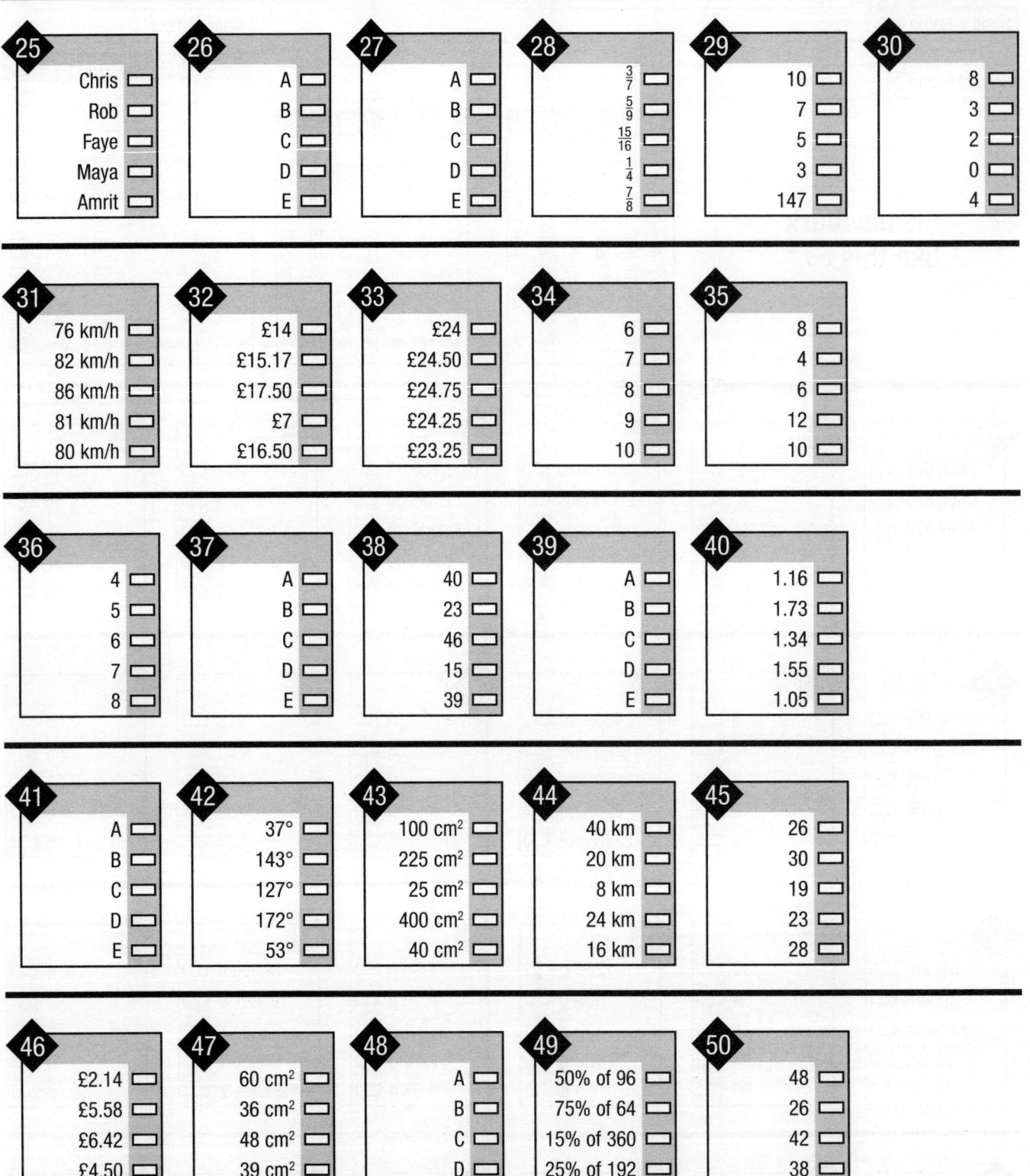